EZGSA Publications, Inc.
PO Box 30406
Bethesda, MD 20824
Phone 301/913-5000 • Fax 301/913-5021

ISBN: 1-4196-3264-7

To order additional copies, please contact
BookSurge, LLC
www.booksurge.com
866/308-6235
orders@booksurge.com

Getting a GSA Schedule

A Step by Step Guide

Scott Orbach
Judith Nelson

Disclaimers

Getting a
GSA Schedule

A Step by Step Guide

TABLE OF CONTENTS

Introduction

CONGRATULATIONS!

By purchasing this book, you have made the first step to expanding your presence in the federal marketplace! And we are pleased to be an integral part of your growth and success.

With more than $33 billion in overall sales during FY2005, the GSA Multiple Award Schedule (MAS), usually referred to as the GSA Schedule, program is a vital procurement tool for the federal government. Marine units are equipped with boots, Hurricane Katrina clean up volunteers sleep under tents, US Customs officials lock containers with bolts, and Veteran's Adminstration hospitals are staffed with temporary professional medical personnel - all using GSA MAS contracts. The information in the following chapters, presented in as jargon free a manner as possible, provides step by step guidance through the process of completing and negotiating a GSA Schedule proposal. We are hopeful that our years of experience preparing and negotiating more than 500 successfully awarded GSA Schedule contracts will set you on the path to a superior GSA MAS contract for your company.

What is a GSA Sched

The General Services Administration, through i
Acquisition Service (FAS) (an entity evolving as the result of the merger of the Federal Supply Service and the Federal Technology Service), is charged with the responsibility to award Multiple Award Schedule (MAS) contracts commonly referred to as the GSA Schedules. GSA Schedules allow commercial businesses to sell, and federal customers to buy, products and services through long-term contracts. These contracts include pre-negotiated pricing, terms, and conditions. They are awarded for a base period of five years, with the potential for three five-year option periods, effectively making them 20 year contracts. (See *Appendix A: GSA Schedules* for a list of all schedules.)

In effect, you can consider your GSA Schedule to be a "fishing license" for some of the billions of dollars available every year in federal procurements: in fiscal year 2005 GSA Schedule sales accounted for more than $33 billion. (See *Appendix B: GSA Sales Report* for additional information.) Ordering Activities across multiple federal agencies are using schedule contracts to meet their growing procurement requirements. In fact, in each of the five years leading up to 2004, GSA Schedule sales increased an average of 23 percent, while overall federal spending increased only about 6.5 percent.

Before You Begin

We strongly suggest that you first determine under which Schedule you belong. To do this, please go to http://www.gsaelibrary.gsa.gov/.

In the "Search" box, enter a few key words that best describe your product or service. These terms should be succinct but encompassing. For instance:

- ☐ "CCTV"
- ☐ "network maintenance"
- ☐ "security guards"
- ☐ "ambulance"
- ☐ "structural engineering consultants"

Once you click "Search", the database will return a page containing a list of all schedule/solicitation documents containing words that match your search criteria. Read through the list to determine under which schedule you best belong.

Remember to download all parts of the solicitation. Depending upon which Schedule you are seeking, the solicitation could download in single or multiple parts (as few as one, as for office furniture; or as many as four, as for information technology).

Before continuing with this guide, we suggest you read the solicitation, underlining or highlighting parts that you don't quite understand. You may also find a number of unfamiliar acronyms both throughout the solicitation and this guide. These are defined in *Appendix C: Common Acronyms.*

Chapter 1
Getting Started

1.1 Overview of the Process

1.1.1 How Long Will It Take?

When EZGSA's proposal specialists work on a client's proposal, they usually follow the time line below. You should strive to achieve these milestones as well.

Estimated Timeline for the Offer Life Cycle

INHOUSE

•Data Collection	4 weeks
•Offer Completion	2 weeks

AT GSA

•Preliminary Review and Assignment of CO	3 weeks
•Administrative Clarifications	12 weeks
•Negotiations	2 weeks
•Final Proposal Revisions	1 week

AWARD!

24 weeks, or
6 months

1.1.2 The Three Rs of Government Contracting

GSA evaluates your company and offer for Responsiveness, Responsibility, and Reasonableness commonly referred to as the Three Rs of contracting.

1.1.2.1 Responsiveness

GSA reviews your offer to ensure that it conforms to all solicitation requirements. Responsiveness can be defined as providing all required information and data in an accurate manner and conforming to solicitation formatting instructions. Many, but not all, of the solicitations currently contain an "Offer Checklist" which can serve as an effective aid for completing and organizing the offer. A submitted offer not responding in sufficient detail to the solicitation's evaluation points is deemed non-responsive and is subject to rejection. It is extremely important to format the offer specifically as per the instructions outlined in the solicitation.

Responsiveness also means replying in a timely manner to GSA requests for additional information or clarifications during the review of your offer. Although GSA Schedule proposals do not have deadlines for submittal, a Contracting Officer (CO) can set a deadline for responses on additional information or clarifications concerning your offer. Failure to submit timely responses to GSA subjects the offer to rejection for non-responsiveness.

1.1.2.2 Responsibility

GSA determines how responsible your company is through a Past Performance Evaluation (PPE). GSA has designated a private company, Open Ratings, to collect reference information from potential Schedule vendors and to use that information to compile its PPE. The Open Ratings questionnaire asks for 10 to 20 past customer references who are then surveyed by Open Ratings via email and asked to rank your company on a scale of zero to ten in a number of performance-related areas. Open Ratings reports the results of their survey to GSA and sends your company a copy as well. (*See Chapter 2 for additional details about Open Ratings reports.*)

GSA requests that companies offering services also describe a few of their past projects that are similar in scope to the services they will offer. Most solicitations ask for two to three projects, completed in the last two years, for each Special Item Number (SIN).

Your company's financial status is another way that GSA determines responsibility. Depending upon the Schedule for which you are applying, this may vary from providing a profit and loss statement and balance statement to three years of audited financial reports. At times, GSA will request further documentation about your financial status and perform a more detailed financial review. (*See Chapter 3 for additional details about financial reviews.*)

1.1.2.3 Reasonableness

Although reasonableness can be a subjective term, GSA measures reasonableness by comparing your proposed GSA pricing to that for your commercial and other customers. GSA will make the determination that your pricing is reasonable based upon multiple factors, but among the most important is the price that the open market has determined to be fair and reasonable. Thus, your proposal will be stronger if your company has definitive & consistent commercial price list(s) already in place, along with a set of standard practices for when and how often discounts and other concessions are granted and to whom, if ever.

Reasonableness should not necessarily imply that the GSA will receive better pricing than any of your other customers. For instance, if your only price break to any customer is a ten percent discount off of commercial pricing with a minimum order of $250,000, then GSA should not automatically expect a ten percent discount unless they also purchase that amount. Similarly, GSA should not expect to benefit from the same discount structure accorded your dealers, who provide promotion and marketing activity, sales force assistance, technical support, tradeshow representation, unit storage, etc.

1.2 Registrations You Will Have to Complete

In order to fully comply with all clauses in the Schedule solicitations, you must register with a few well-known entities and complete a few not-so-well-known reports. These are described below.

1.2.1 Dun & Bradstreet (D&B)

D&B is an international company that maintains credit histories on companies. GSA requires that your company register with D&B and receive a DUNS number from them. This number is the widely recognized standard for identifying companies in the commercial marketplace. GSA will verify that the corporate address you provide in your proposal matches that of your D&B files. To apply for or find out your DUNS number, go to the *Dun & Bradstreet* link at http://www.ezgsa.com/sub_links/dsp_links.shtml.

1.2.2 NAICS/SIC Codes

The federal government uses the North American Industry Classification System (NAICS) codes to categorize each industry and line of business whether manufacturing, wholesaling, service provider or retailer. NAICS replaced Standard Industrial Classification (SIC) codes more than five years ago with the introduction of the North American Free Trade Act (NAFTA), but some COs may still ask for both codes as does the CCR (see below).

One of the most important uses of the NAICS standards is the size standard. The federal government determines per NAICS code (business classification) a standard for small business size. It is interesting to note that as of January 6, 2006, the Small Business Administration (SBA) increased the size standards 7.8% (for an inflationary adjustment) for the first time since 2002. To determine your company's NAICS and/or SIC code, you should check the Small Business Administration's NAICS/SIC search. This can be accessed via the *NAICS/SIC Code Identification and Search* link at http://www.ezgsa.com/sub_links/dsp_links.shtml.

1.2.3 Central Contractor Registration (CCR)

The CCR is the "primary vendor database for the U.S. federal government" (*CCR Handbook, May 2004*). Although registration is free, all current and potential government contractors (ergo, all companies applying for a GSA Schedule contract) must register with CCR and update the registration yearly.

CCR registration requires that you already have a DUNS number (see above). Registration includes fields for your company's basic information, including: business location; business type; NAICS codes; and points of contact for administration, sales, and marketing. (See *Appendix D: CCR Handbook, May 2004 version* for additional information.)

Upon successfully completing the registration, CCR will mail you a Trading Partner Identification Number (TPIN) so that you can access the site for updating your company's profile. The TPIN will never be shown on any contract or purchase order and should only be requested by the government or any entity for the specific purpose of updating your CCR profile. The TPIN will be mailed through the U.S. Postal Service to your company's designated point of contact. You should file it in a safe and secure place, but one that you can find.

1.2.4 Marketing Partner Identification Number (MPIN)

You create your MPIN code when you register in CCR. The MPIN also allows you to access other government applications such as the Online Representations and Certifications Application (ORCA), the Past Performance Information Retrieval System (PPIRS), FedBizOpps, and FedTeDS.

1.2.5 Online Representations and Certifications Application (ORCA)

The government intends ORCA to replace hard copy Representations and Certifications. Although at this point you must still submit the "Reps and Certs" with your GSA Schedule proposal, GSA is requiring all potential government vendors to also complete the ORCA process. Once you have received your MPIN, go to the *ORCA* link at http://www.ezgsa.com/sub_links/dsp_links.shtml.

We urge you to print the pages you complete for your ORCA registration, and check that they match the "Reps and Certs" in your GSA Schedule proposal.

1.2.6 Taxpayer Identification Number (TIN)

The Internal Revenue Service (IRS) uses your company's TIN for collecting taxes and administering tax laws. Other government agencies use the TIN to report certain contract information (e.g., contracts and modifications in excess of $25,000) as well as payment information to the IRS. A TIN is issued either by the Social Security Administration or by the IRS.

1.2.7 VETS-100 Report

VETS-100 is a continuing effort by the government to encourage private-sector businesses to hire and promote qualified veterans. Businesses with a federal contract worth $25,000 or more must complete a VETS-100 Report. This simple two-page form demonstrates, among other things, the number of targeted veterans in your company by job category, hiring location, and new hires. The government asks for this data for informational purposes only, not for enforcement. Penalties do not accrue to companies without veterans on the payroll. Instructions, information, and further assistance can be found at the *VETS-100 Fact Sheet* or *VETS-100 Reporting* links at http://www.ezgsa.com/sub_links/dsp_links.shtml.

Chapter 2
Data Collection & Proposal Production

This chapter provides helpful information, insights, and references for some of the various data items you will need in order to complete your GSA Schedule proposal.

2.1 General Data Collection

This is data that will be requested in all GSA Schedule solicitations, whether you are proposing to provide products or services. If you are a veteran government contractor, most of this will be quite familiar.

2.1.1 Standard Form 1449 (SF1449)

Each GSA Schedule proposal includes an SF1449 as its opening page. On this form, you will need to enter the payment terms you are offering the government, your company's name and address (which should match the address in your DUNS and CCR records), your company's phone and fax numbers, and your company's DUNS number. A company official will also be required to sign and date the document.

2.1.2 Addresses

GSA requires that the corporate address listed in the proposal match the address as registered with both

Dun & Bradstreet and CCR. You may list different physical addresses for payment, ordering, and service provision.

2.1.3 Contract Administrator

This is a person within your company who will be responsible for all the paperwork associated with your GSA contract once it has been awarded. S/he will be the primary point of contact for the GSA Administrative Contracting Officer assigned to your company. If you intend to offer your products and/or services worldwide, you must designate a Contract Administrator in each region of the world, e.g., the Pacific Rim, Europe, and the Middle East.

2.1.4 Business Size and Type

Is your company a small business? The Small Business Administration (SBA) sets standards that companies must meet to qualify as a "small business." These standards vary by industry and are organized according to NAICS codes. The definitions utilized by SBA can be found at the *Small Business Size Standards* link at http://www.ezgsa.com/sub_links/dsp_links.shtml.

SIN = Special Item Number

As a side note, some SINs are set aside for small businesses, which means that only small businesses may be awarded contracts to provide those services. Some examples include the SINs for snow maintenance equipment, security applications for business machines, transportation audits, web-based marketing services, and above ground storage tanks.

Further details about size determination are described below.

Affiliates - A company's size determination is made when accounting for the employees or receipts of all offices as well as all affiliates. Affiliation is defined as the power to control, whether exercised or not. Factors such as common ownership, common management, and identity of interest (often found in members of the same family), among others, are indicators of affiliation. Power to control exists when a party or parties have 50 percent or more ownership. It may also exist with considerably less than 50 percent ownership by contractual arrangement or when one or more parties own a large share compared to other parties. Affiliated business concerns need not have the same line of business (see *Small Business Administration Size Standards* link at http://www.ezgsa.com/sub_links/dsp_links.shtml for more information).

Annual Receipts - SBA determines a company's gross receipts by averaging total revenue for the last three completed fiscal years. Net capital gains or losses are not generally included in this calculation.

Employees - This is reported as the average number of individuals employed for each pay period over the company's last 12 months. All employees, even temporary and part-time, are included in this calculation (see *Small Business Administration Size Standards* link at http://www.ezgsa.com/sub_links/dsp_links.shtml for more information).

2.1.4.1 8(a) Business Development Program

SBA created this program for small businesses owned by socially and economically disadvantaged individuals. Firms admitted to the program can receive federal contracts designated for 8(a) Business Development Program participants as well as management and technical assistance (see SDB Program below).

2.1.4.2 HUBZone

The Historically Underutilized Business Zone (HUBZone) Empowerment Contracting Program is meant to stimulate economic development and create jobs in urban and rural communities. HUBZone businesses reside in these identified areas and are owned and controlled by one or more U.S. citizens or a Community Development Corporation or an Indian tribe. Additionally, at least 35 percent of all employees must be residents of the HUBZone area. SBA certifies businesses as HUBZone eligible and maintains a listing of qualified HUBZone small businesses that federal agencies can use to locate prospective vendors. To find out if your company is located in a HUBZone, refer to the *HUBZone Map* at http://www.ezgsa.com/sub_links/dsp_links.shtml.

2.1.4.3 Small Disadvantaged Business (SDB) Program

While the 8(a) Business Development Program (above) offers a broad scope of assistance to socially and economically disadvantaged concerns, SDB certification strictly pertains to benefits in federal procurement. SDB certification is automatically awarded to all 8(a) companies. Special bidding benefits exist for SDBs, and prime contractors receive credit for utilizing SDBs as subcontractors.

If you still have questions about your business size, please see the *Small Business Administration FAQ* link at http://www.ezgsa.com/sub_links/dsp_links.shtml.

2.2 Schedule Specific Data Collection

Each GSA Schedule solicitation includes data requirements that are specific to that particular product or service. Your company's offer may or may not require the data described in this section, so be sure to read the solicitation completely before collecting the information described below.

2.2.1 Requirements in Both Product and Service Schedules

2.2.1.1 Special Item Numbers (SINs)

Each GSA Schedule organizes its products and services into manageable categories, or SINs. For example, GSA Schedule 70 (Information Technology Products and Professional Services) includes the following 12 SINs:

SIN 132-3	Leasing of products
SIN 132-4	Daily/short term rental
SIN 132-8	Purchase of equipment
SIN 132-12	Equipment maintenance
SIN 132-32	Term software license
SIN 132-33	Perpetual software license
SIN 132-34	Software maintenance
SIN 132-50	Classroom training

SIN 132-51 Information technology services

SIN 132-52 Electronic commerce services

SIN 132-53 Wireless services

SIN 132-60 Authentication products and services

You may only offer the products and/or professional services to GSA that you already provide in the commercial marketplace. This should fall into just a few SINs, especially if you propose only your core business products or services. The fewer SINs offered, the speedier your administrative review and award process. Remember, you can always modify your schedule and add on other products or services at a later date.

2.2.1.2 Brochures/Catalogs

Brochures describing a company's products and services are welcome, although you should ensure that the brochure actually describes the offerings to be included on the Schedule and not tangential information. Additionally, GSA does require that any commercial catalogs of your company's products or services, including pricing, be submitted with the Schedule proposal. Contracting Officers at a few of the acquisition centers also wish to see the commercial catalog from your previous fiscal year.

2.2.1.3 Ordering Method

GSA requests that vendors provide either Electronic Data Interchange (EDI) access or a fax number for government orders. For EDI, your company must have a FACNET-certified Value Added Network (VAN) provider. If you are considering this option, ensure that your VAN has the necessary conversion software.

EDI is further described in *Appendix E: FIPS PUB 161-2*. Should you elect to use EDI as the ordering method, GSA asks for a contact's name, address, and telephone number for initiating the interface.

2.2.1.4 Government Credit Card Acceptance

All GSA Schedule contracts require the awardee to accept government-wide commercial credit cards for purchases of $2,500 or under. (See reference to the micro-purchase threshold in *Appendix F: FAR 2.101, Micro-Purchase Threshold*). If your company does not currently accept credit cards as payment, you will still be required to offer this option to government buyers. Be sure that

the credit card merchant you sel[illegible]
government purchase cards.

Although not required, GSA enc[illegible]
contractors to accept government purchase
card orders exceeding the micro-purchase
threshold. Regulations state that payments
by credit card can be processed only after the
product shipment or the service performance.

Please note that when the government pays by credit card, the ordering agency is *not* eligible for a prompt payment discount. When the government pays by debit card, the ordering agency *is* eligible for a prompt payment discount.

2.2.1.5 Delivery Times

Most often, GSA defines normal delivery times for products as being 30 to 45 calendar days after receipt of order (ARO). Your company should offer a delivery time based on your normal expected delivery in the commercial sector. Delivery times can vary for quantity orders as necessary, but should be pre-defined.

For products, this means that the normal delivery of the item to the FOB (free on board) point is within the dates you establish.

ARO =
After Receipt of Offer

When defining delivery times for services requiring a Statement of Work (SOW) it is standard to state that delivery will be negotiated on a task order basis between the Ordering Activity and the contractor.

GSA also wants to know if your company is available to provide the products/services proposed in an expedited manner. If you offer expedited service for your business in the commercial marketplace, then you should also offer this to the government.

2.2.1.6 Geographic Areas

The geographic scope for all GSA schedules is worldwide. However, GSA allows companies to limit the geographic area in which they will provide products and services at the prices, terms, and conditions of their GSA Schedule. The two geographic options GSA allows are:

CONUS

Domestic

Domestic delivery can be either within the 48 Continental United States and District of Columbia (CONUS) or beyond CONUS, which includes Alaska, Hawaii, and U.S. territories such as Puerto Rico, US Virgin Islands, Guam, and Saipan.

Some Schedules, i.e. the information technology schedule, require a minimum geographic coverage of CONUS. Others, such as the facilities maintenance schedule, allow contractors to limit the geographic scope to specific areas within the country.

International - Foreign countries

For international delivery, GSA requires that your company actually have a contact (with local address and phone number) in those regions where you wish to provide products/services. For instance, if your company will be selling software to U.S. military bases in Germany, then a contact name with phone number and address in Germany must be given. These can be provided in a separate list.

Unless your company has set offices or sales representatives in foreign countries, we suggest that you provide domestic delivery only. Limiting the geographic area to domestic in a GSA Schedule does not preclude your company from providing products or services in a geographic area outside the U.S. An ordering officer in Germany can always contact his/her domestic agency for ordering.

Companies that ship products often wish

to limit the geographic scope to domestic because:

- Most GSA schedules require that the price for products offered under a GSA schedule include FOB Destination shipment, which is more costly and risky for overseas delivery.
- Labor or service cost differentials exist in foreign countries.
- Even if you are able to separate pricing by country and geographic area (although all pricing must be in U.S. dollars), managing and maintaining these different prices can be difficult.
- Companies providing domestic scope orders only are held to GSA pricing, terms, and conditions for domestic orders only.

2.2.2 Requirements for Product Schedules

2.2.2.1 Buy American Act - Trade Agreements

Any company selling products through the GSA Schedules must comply with the Buy American Act - Trade Agreements (FAR 52.225-5, which can be seen in *Appendix G: Trade Agreements*). The end product you sell must be made in either the U.S., a designated country, a Caribbean Basin country, or a NAFTA (North American Free Trade Agreement) country. For instance, a manufacturer with clock factories in both China and Mexico would only be allowed to offer on the GSA Schedule those clocks made in Mexico. Please see *Appendix G* for additional details on this section as well as a list of authorized, designated countries.

2.2.2.2 Hazardous Materials, Safety Standards, and EPA Registration

Items that you are offering with possible fire or casualty hazards (e.g., items containing electrical components), or safety or health requirements, must conform to any safety standards issued by a nationally recognized standards developing organization or the

EPA itself. In the section requesting this information, please identify the actual standards and be prepared to provide proof that your products conform to these standards. Acceptable proof includes labeling, listing, or acceptance of the product by an organization approved by the Occupational Safety and Health Administration (OSHA) as a Nationally Recognized Testing Laboratory (NRTL). Please include a list with the hazardous material name, identification number, and Material Safety Data Sheet.

2.2.2.3 Production and Inspection Points

In your solicitation, GSA asks for the production and inspection point addresses of all offered products. Manufacturers should be able to provide this information easily. Resellers may need to ask the manufacturer for this data. Often, production and inspection occur at the same address, and this should be indicated if it is the case. Note: this section requests not only the street address, but also the county.

2.2.2.4 FOB Delivery

Generally, FOB concerns the delivery of your products. The four most common choices for

FOB include the following (see *Appendix H: FAR FOB Terms* for detailed descriptions):

FOB Origin (FAR 52.247-29)

Used for domestic shipment. Delivery is made to a designated point in the city from which the shipment originates, and the shipper is responsible for any loss of and/or damage to the goods occurring before delivery to the carrier, including from improper packing and marking.

FOB Destination (FAR 52.247-34)

Also for domestic shipment. The preferred option for domestic CONUS delivery on most Schedules, this means that the price you offer GSA includes delivery, free of expense to the government, to a government-designated facility. The shipper is responsible for any loss of and/or damage to the goods occurring before delivery.

FOB Inland Carrier, Country of Exportation (FAR 52.247-38)

Used for international shipment. Your GSA offered price includes delivery, free of expense to the government, on an inland carrier, to the specified point of exportation. You are responsible for any loss of and/or damage to the goods occurring before delivery to the specified point of exportation. At the government's expense, you may be requested to assist in obtaining the documents required for exportation or importation at destination.

FOB Inland Point, Country of Importation (FAR 52.247-39)

Also for international shipment. Your GSA offered price includes delivery, free of expense to the government, to the specified inland point where the buyer's facility is located. The shipper is responsible for any loss of and/or damage to the goods occurring before delivery to the inland point. The shipper pays and bears all applicable charges incurred up to the point of delivery, including transportation costs; export, import, or other fees or taxes; costs of landing; wharfage costs; customs duties and costs of certificates of origin; consular invoices; and other documents that may be required for importation.

2.2.2.5 Letters of Supply

Most product Schedules require that

companies selling products they themselves do not manufacture obtain a Letter of Supply/Commitment from the manufacturer or a supplier. Your company must have a guaranteed source for the products you are offering. (See *Appendix I: Example Letter of Supply*)

2.2.3 Service Schedules

Service solicitations' responses are generally divided into three distinct proposal sections. These are: the Administrative, the Technical, and the Pricing Proposals. The Administrative Proposal is the completed base solicitation and appropriate attachments. The Technical Proposal is comprised of the executive summary, past performance project descriptions, corporate experience, professional compensation plan summary, quality control plan, and other solicitation specific requirements. The Pricing Proposal includes the commercial sales practices chart (CSP-1), your commercial and proposed GSA price lists, a statement regarding uncompensated overtime, and all required back-up documentation for your pricing.

2.2.3.1 Company Overview or Executive Summary

Usually a one-page summary, this introduces the GSA Contracting Officer to your company and your core business. Many companies use text from an annual report or the "About Us" section of their website, but previous proposals' executive summaries work just as well. The summary should include a brief history of your company, the date the company was established, years of experience in providing the services being offered, and number of employees. We suggest that you also incorporate (in a general manner) work performed previously that is similar to this Schedule's requirements.

Some Schedules may require that you address additional points in your company overview. Please read the requirements under the Technical Proposal portion of your solicitation closely.

2.2.3.2 Company Organizational Chart

This illustrative depiction of your company's management structure should include the title of management or supervisory personnel as well as all divisions/departments of the company that you expect to be involved in the performance of your GSA Schedule.

2.2.3.3 Past Performance Project Descriptions

GSA requires that each SIN for which you are applying be accompanied by descriptions about successful client projects and contact information for those clients. The number of past performance project descriptions required varies according to the solicitation. For instance, IT Services asks for three per SIN; MOBIS asks for two; Professional Engineering asks for one. The number of past performance project descriptions required will be listed in your solicitation under the Technical Proposal portion.

Past performance project descriptions are extremely important in the service Schedules. Uninformative or incomplete descriptions could cause the rejection of your entire proposal. GSA checks to verify that your projects are similar in scope to the service you propose to provide; that the project has been completed within the past two years (a few of the Schedules allow ongoing projects to be listed); and that your objectives, methodology, and results are described in detail. Other facts, such as both estimated and actual dates of service, a contact name, phone number, and email address as well as dollar amounts of the contract must be included.

Most solicitations require that you are specific about the service and project so that the CO can evaluate your ability to perform similar services for government agencies under your GSA Schedule contract. However, you must be aware of the solicitation's Statement of Work. If you are submitting a proposal under the Advertising and Integrated Marketing Services solicitation, for example, your past performance project descriptions should not include extraneous information about coding the back end of databases. If you are submitting a proposal under the MOBIS solicitation, you may only provide descriptions for past projects in which you provided business improvement methodologies. For example, providing training on project management is acceptable under this solicitation while actual project management is not.

2.2.3.4 Labor Category Descriptions

When providing services, you will give the government a list of your standard commercial labor categories. For instance, a facilities maintenance contract may include the following labor categories: Airplane Mechanic I, Airplane Mechanic II, Project Director, Program Manager, Scheduler.

Professional labor category descriptions must include the name of the category, years of experience required, degree and/or certifications required, and a paragraph describing the position's functional responsibilities. When writing these descriptions, keep in mind that the CO will want to see that the positions support the Statement of Work. Some solicitations permit support personnel, such as administrative assistants, to be included as long as they assist in performing the tasks described in the SIN and are purchased only in conjunction with the professional labor categories. By definition a Schedule contract is a non-personal contract. That is, at the time of award of the base contract, GSA is awarding the labor categories themselves, but is not considering which individuals will perform under the contract. Nonetheless, a few solicitations require resumes of key personnel in order to better assess a company's expertise in functional areas.

When proposing non-professional labor categories, you need not provide full descriptions, only the labor category titles. (All non-professional labor performed under the Schedule contract must comply with the Service Contract Act (SCA) Wage Determinations. This subject will be covered in greater depth in the pricing section.)

2.2.3.5 Quality Control Plan

Many of the service solicitations ask companies to share their quality control plans. This should be a detailed description of the methodology your company follows to ensure that the work performed for your clients meets expectations.

Some of the points that the solicitation asks you to discuss include: how your company provides at least one level of managerial review; what corrective and preventive measures your company takes with a project; how you provide appropriate training to employees and subcontractors; the way in which your company handles multiple task orders and organizational conflicts of interest; and procedures for meeting urgent requirements.

2.2.3.6 Uncompensated Overt Professional Compensation P

If you have a formal written pol with overtime pay, uncompensated overtime, and employee benefits, GSA will need a copy. Those companies without a formal written policy will need to provide a written explanation covering how the company pays overtime, procedures for salaried personnel, and a description of the benefits provided to employees (e.g., health insurance, 401K program). Please see *Appendix J: Uncompensated Overtime and Professional Compensation FAR Clauses* for further information.

2.3 Commercial Sales Practices (CSPs)

Your company's commercial sales and discounting practices comprise the core of your pricing submission. As your offer is being made on a supply basis and is not being compared to a competitor for a particular procurement requirement, the government evaluates your proposed pricing in relationship to the pricing you make available to other customers. The CSP chart is the summary mechanism for these pricing disclosures.

.3.1 Classes of Customers

Companies selling products are likely to have more classes of customers than companies selling services. Furthermore, classes vary according to your type of company: Are you a manufacturer or a reseller? Do you have dealers? Have you only sold your services to state governments?

Below is the list of different customer classes, as well as some reasons why these classes sometimes receive pricing concessions.

2.3.1.1 Dealer/Distributor

Manufacturers of products often utilize dealers and distributors to get their products to the general public. In most companies, the distribution process involves two tiers. That is, the manufacturer sells to a stocking distributor who sells to a reseller, who then sells to the end user. Some dealers and distributors sell to both resellers and end users. Distributor or channel discounts are often predicated on the level of commitment, e.g., the dealer is required to stock product, attend trade shows, provide first level warranty service, participate in Marketing Development Fund activities and sign a channel partner agreement.

2.3.1.2 Value Added Reseller (V and System Integrators (SI)

VARs (generally for products) and SIs (generally for services) also receive discounts from a manufacturer because they take the manufacturer's product and increase its value by adding specific applications; ultimately the manufacturer's product is purchased by the VAR/SI and then re-sold to the general public at a price that includes the increased value. Manufacturers discount their products to a VAR /SI because the VAR/SI will actually change the product and therefore offer for sale a product that costs more to the end user.

2.3.1.3 Reseller

Resellers purchase goods from a manufacturer at wholesale prices and then sell the goods to customers unchanged for a higher price. For the wholesale price discount, the reseller often provides customer service such as billing to the client, or purchases in bulk.

2.3.1.4 Original Equipment Manufacturer (OEMs)

OEMs enter into agreements with manufacturers to relabel products under their own brand. This class receives discounts because under their branding, they sell a manufacturer's production to a wider customer base. OEMs cannot offer customers a pass-through of the original manufacturer's

warranty, but as the "brand" must offer their own warranty and terms.

2.3.1.5 Non-Profit

Tax exempt, non-profit organizations provide products or services to the community and receive payment for those services. However, after expenses, all revenue is funneled back into the organization for re-investment.

Businesses that sell to non-profits at a discount often receive a tax deduction for doing so or offer the discounts as part of the business's own community involvement.

2.3.1.6 Educational Institutions

Many businesses also provide discounts to schools and universities for a number of reasons, not the least of which may be to assist in the promotion of learning or as another facet of the business' community involvement. Nevertheless, GSA does separate educational institutions from non-profits.

2.3.1.7 State and Local Governments

Your pricing to state and/or local governments may be discounted due to long-term contracts, work that's been competitively bid, or other reasons.

2.3.1.8 National Accounts

National accounts are large corporate entities with a single procurement authority such as Hilton Hotels or IBM. These large corporations can leverage their size to negotiate greater discounts from vendors. Many COs believe that GSA most closely mirrors the national account class of customer.

2.3.1.9 Commercial End Users

In reality, most businesses find that their GSA pricing is tied to the commercial end user class. If 85 percent of your revenue is from commercial end users, your discounting practices with this class will be most important to your negotiations with the CO.

2.3.1.10 Federal Government

Many acquisition offices prefer that you not include discounts to the federal government in the CSP chart; nevertheless, there are some cases in which it behooves your company's negotiation strategy to do so. For instance, the company that had 100 percent of its last fiscal year revenue from federal government sources and never discounted could be in a good position to go into negotiations offering a 0 percent discount for Schedule pricing.

2.3.1.11 International

Unless you are also offering international delivery to GSA, this class of customer would not affect your GSA Schedule pricing.

2.3.1.12 Prime Contractors

Most subcontractors offer their prime a discounted rate, which the prime then increases to approximately the same as the original, non-discounted rate for the government client. Therefore, the end client (the government) will not be receiving a discount off of the subcontractor's rates. Moreover, most subcontractors are not privy to the billing rate primes charge for their services.

2.3.2 Best Customer Discount

In the CSP chart, GSA requires that you disclose the customer classes to which you offer a discount. Some Schedules require that you provide an actual client name as well. This may be a one-time discount or an ongoing discount. You must list the following information:

- Class of customer (e.g., Commercial End Users; Distributors)
- Standard discount provided (e.g., No discount ever; 2% on wire accessories when base unit is purchased; 10% across the board discount)
- Quantity/Volume (e.g. $500,000 per purchase order receives 6% discount off list price; 100 units of same line item receive 2 free units; 1,080 hours of a labor category receives 0.5% discount)
- Concessions (e.g., customers active for five years receive free beta versions; contract terms were 2% net 20).

It may be that you provide a discount for a particular product or labor category on a particular project, but not for any other line item on any other project. Unless that discount occurred more than one year ago and it is no longer ongoing, you must disclose it. The manner in which you disclose - and justify - these discounts, will begin to establish your GSA pricing and negotiating strategy.

to GSA

should be developed based on (1) your
| sales practices, and (2) your discounting
...ass of customer similar to the GSA customer. All items offered on the GSA Schedule must have an established, fixed unit price. Your pricing can be adjusted through official modifications after award, but for the purposes of obtaining your GSA Schedule listing, you must submit a definitive, quantifiable price list.

One of the most common mistakes made by GSA Schedule applicants is to submit pricing based on already awarded GSA Schedule contract pricing instead of on their own commercial sales practices. The awarded pricing is a ceiling sale price to the government buyer. That is, for competitive reasons, you may choose to offer a government buyer a lower price than your awarded one. You can always easily decrease your Schedule pricing after award, but increases are much more limited. The strategy of obtaining an award based on your regular pricing, and then discounting when necessary to remain competitive, is the more sound approach.

As noted above, there are a number of different classes of customers. You may sell to all these classes, to five of these classes, or to one. The tricky part is to know to which class of customer to tie your GSA pricing.

When the contract is awarded, the pricing will be

established as a relationship to a specific class of customer. So if you and the government agree that the Basis of Award is the commercial end user class of customer, the GSA pricing will forever be tied to changes that occur to to the commercial end user pricing. If your company reduces its prices to the commercial end user or changes its policy of granting discounts and allows greater discounts, you will automatically be on the hook to give those discounts to GSA. If the end user prices increase, you will be entitled to request price increases of GSA though you are not guaranteed to receive the full amount.

It is important to make full and accurate disclosures to GSA on the Commercial Sales Practices chart. However while GSA may ask for Most Favored Customer (MFC) pricing, you should only offer MFC pricing to them for a class of customer with similar terms and conditions. If distributors receive a 40% discount because they stock product, provide warranty claim service, attend trade shows, demonstrate new products, and have minimum volume sales requirements, they have very different terms then those of the GSA Schedule. In this case, you should not offer to GSA your distributor pricing. Likewise, if you offer commercial end users a 10% discount for a volume purchase of 40 units you may only want to offer the GSA this 10% discount for a similar volume commitment.

There are some other significant issues or circumstances that you should examine before proposing your pricing. A few common examples are:

- You are the subcontractor to a prime government contractor. Your subcontract rates are approximately 25 percent lower than your commercially advertised and otherwise accepted rates. However, the prime contractor sells your services to the government for your full commercial rate. You believe you must offer GSA the subcontract rate.
- You provide a discount to a long-time client who purchases over $1 million in products per year. You believe you must offer GSA the same discount for all purchases.
- You have a contract negotiated more than two years ago, wherein your pricing is discounted from your current rates. You believe you must offer GSA these same rates.
- You sell only to distributors and dealers, and not to commercial end users. You believe you must offer GSA the distributor and dealer rates.
- Your product pricing for commercial customers is always FOB Origin but the particular GSA Schedule for which you are applying requires FOB Destination. You believe you must offer GSA pricing at or

below the pricing that you give your FOB Origin commercial customers.

- You have granted significant discounts to clients who have served as beta testers or third party validators, and you think you must grant the government these large discounts as well.

Your pricing strategy should be considered fully and discussed with multiple members of your company, including your Chief Financial Officer, contract managers (who maintain contracts already awarded), and project and sales managers (who do the actual work or discount the actual products in the field). Research all your discounting practices over the past year or so. Talk to your Research and Development departments or individuals to discover for what types of projects you will be applying in the near future and how they will approach pricing on these projects. Most important of all, make certain that the pricing you are submitting is pricing you can live with. Although you can modify your contract to add and delete line items, these changes will always be tied to the class of customer you have already negotiated for your Schedule. Modifying or changing that relationship is difficult.

2.4.1 Commercial Price List

2.4.1.1 Products

GSA requests that you submit either a current

commercial catalog or commercial price list with your proposal. A few special requirements apply depending on your type of business: for instance, manufacturers with no sales to the general public should include an MSRP price list; resellers of audio visual or information technology equipment will be required to demonstrate their purchase price from the wholesaler so that GSA can determine the mark-up.

Additionally, some schedules (such as those from the Ft. Worth acquisition center) require that you also submit a commercial price list from your previous fiscal year.

If you are including a commercial catalog, you must cross out any items or pages that are not listed on your GSA Schedule price list.

2.4.1.2 Services

If you are proposing professional services you will be required to justify your proposed rates by one of two methods. GSA's preferred method is through pricing back up. Using this method, you would provide ample (defined as one to three) commercial invoices or signed agreements showing that the labor categories as proposed have been sold and accepted at the

pricing you are proposing to the
The other method of justifying y
cost build up; that is, to provide
from direct rates with Overhead,
a proposed Fee to a final billable rate. If you have an audited Overhead and G&A from the Defense Contract Audit Agency (DCAA) or another government auditing entity then you should provide the documentation with your rate build-up.

If you are proposing non-professional services, you are bound by the Service Contract Act (SCA) labor categories. You must pay all workers the minimum wage and health and welfare amount as determined for each jurisdiction by the appropriate SCA Wage Determination. You will show the government a rate build up from the SCA wage with health and welfare, uniforms, labor burden, corporate overhead, and a negotiable fee. For additional information, visit *Wage Determinations OnLine.gov* at http://www.wdol.gov.

2.4.2 GSA Price list

Your GSA Price list should include all of the following items:

□ Header with company name, effective date, and SIN. (If proposing one SIN, then the SIN should be in the header. If you are proposing to provide more than one SIN, you should include a column specifically designated for listing the SIN.)

☐ Columns including:

- o SIN (see note above)
- o Item/Labor category name
- o Item description (if applicable)
- o Part number (if applicable)
- o Commercial price
- o Discount offered to GSA in percentage
- o Discount offered to GSA in dollars
- o Basic GSA price
- o Industrial Funding Fee (IFF) - see discussion below
- o Final GSA price
- o Country of manufacture (if applicable)

☐ A separate matrix for across the board quantity and/or volume discounts

2.4.2.1 Industrial Funding Fee (IFF)

The IFF is a fee equal to 0.75 percent of every sale you make through your GSA Schedule contract. This fee is meant to allow the GSA to recoup its operating costs from Ordering Activities; indeed, the IFF makes GSA a profit center for the government.

Potential GSA Schedule contractor
include the IFF in their final prices.
included in your award prices and is reflected in the total amount charged to Ordering Activities.

This means that after you have calculated your proposed discount to the government you will then add on (mark up) your price with a factor for the IFF. The actual factor for calculation purposes is 0.00756. Below is a simple example assuming you have a product that sells commercially for $100.00 that you are offering to the government at a 10% discount.

LIST PRICE	$100.00
DISCOUNT 10%	
GSA PRICE	$90.00
IFF	$0.68
FINAL GSA PRICE	$90.68

There are three exceptions to the ¾% IFF fee. Under the VA/FSS solicitations the IFF fee for medical supplies is 0.5%, and for professional medical services the IFF fee is 1%. For those who are offering travel services, the IFF fee is $1.50 per transaction.

2.4.2.2 Discounts

Discounts should be listed in the discounting

column. Please note that GSA doesn't necessarily expect you to offer the same discount for every item or labor category.

2.4.2.3 Tax

Because you will be selling to government entities through the Schedule, you cannot add a sales tax to your pricing. This is covered in the FAR, 29.302, which states, "Generally, purchases and leases made by the federal government are immune from state and local taxation."

2.4.2.4 International Companies/Pricing

All pricing must be noted in American dollars.

2.4.2.5 Fair and Reasonable Pricing

As you read through your solicitation, you will see the term "fair and reasonable" repeated time and again. Part of the way in which GSA evaluates your submission is by determining if you offer fair and reasonable pricing. It may seem as if this is quite a subjective term, and it is. However, there are a few guidelines to follow when you are asked to explain in writing why your pricing is fair and reasonable. (This happens almost exclusively in the service solicitations, although the question may arise during discussions with a CO about a product solicitation.)

In your written narrative, keep the information on topic. The CO is tasked with discovering how adequate and realistic are your submitted prices. Supporting documentation that demonstrates that you have billed at or above the pricing proposed for the GSA Schedule boosts your case, as do published price lists, signed agreements, and invoices. In some cases, you may want to discuss your cost build up.

It is unwise to compare your pricing to competitors because there may be another business offering a lower price on some item or service than you are. Differing circumstances such as location, product age and quality, and shipping may not be included in one of your competitor's prices, so you may be opening a can of worms by inviting comparisons.

2.4.3 Supporting and Other Required Documents

2.4.3.1 Invoices, Contracts, and Memoranda of Understanding (MOUs)

As noted above, supporting documentation

will help you to prove that your pricing is fair and reasonable. These documents include invoices for your labor categories or items sold, commercial catalogs displaying your stated commercial pricing, contracts with either government or commercial organizations, and MOUs.

Before bundling these items into your submission, we strongly suggest that you analyze each invoice, contract, or MOU to ensure that the noted rates are the same or higher than your stated commercial pricing. Again, you should be aware that GSA requires a minimum of three invoices per labor category for almost all of the service solicitations.

Please note: those proposing IT Services will be required to provide invoices from the past projects described in the proposal. You should also include a chart displaying the labor categories' commercial prices, pricess offered to GSA, and each past project's price.

2.4.3.2 Defense Contract Audit Agency (DCAA) Audit

If you have been contracting with the federal government for awhile, it is possible that you have undergone a DCAA audit. An agency of the Department of Defense, DCAA audits ongoing contracts to ensure compliance with both financial and contractual obligations. These audits evaluate the policies, procedures, controls, performance, financial capability, and cost structures of a contractor.

DCAA rate approval means that they agree that the costs and indirect rates you charge are allowable, reasonable and allocable. If DCAA has audited and approved your labor rates, you may include the DCAA letter with your proposal. Your pricing should not exceed the approved DCAA audited rates unless significant changes in your company's infrastructure and pricing structure have occurred since the audit. In any case, GSA will require that you explain in writing any pricing differences in excess of those

rates, so you should have this explanation ready to submit when you deliver your proposal.

2.4.3.3 Financial Statements

Some of the product solicitations and all of the service solicitations require company financials be included with your proposal. Most often, you need only include a simple year-to-date profit and loss statement as well as a bank balance.

Some solicitations (e.g., the Financial and Business Services Schedule - FABS) ask that your company include one to three years of independently prepared financials. Large companies are required to submit audited financials more often than small businesses.

2.4.3.4 Subcontracting Plan

All large businesses (determined by the schedule SIN and NAICS code for the products or services being offered) that receive a contract expected to exceed $500,000 must submit a Small Business Subcontracting Plan. Even if you are a small business on some of the SINs you are offering but large on others, you will probably have to complete a subcontracting plan. The general rule is that if you are a large business on one SIN being offered, you are considered a large business for the entire solicitation. (See *Appendix K: Example Subcontracting Plan Format.*)

2.4.3.5 Open Ratings Report

Almost all solicitations require you to submit an Open Ratings report, which is a performance rating survey from 10 to 20 of your clients. A company called Open Ratings, Inc. performs the survey. You must complete the forms included with your solicitation and send them to Open Ratings before you submit the proposal to GSA.

Before providing your list of past customer contacts, you should verify your references' contact information. Open Ratings has recently automated much of their data collection; whereas two years ago they often called references to perform the interviews, they now contact references exclusively by email. However, if you submit six references and only two reply, Open Ratings will be unable to complete your report and your proposal will be delayed at GSA.

We encourage you to use references who will provide positive responses to Open Ratings because a low overall score can result in delays in contract award, and, in some cases, conditions placed on your award.

Open Ratings calculates your performance scores using an algorithm that takes into account the amount of information available on you, how recent the information is, and the accuracy of the raters. Ratings range from zero to 100. However, this is not a percentile score. The survey gathers ratings from your past customer contacts in areas such as reliability, cost containment, order accuracy, delivery timeliness, customer service, staff's professionalism, responsiveness, and overall business relationship.

2.4 Proposal Production

After you have completed your final draft, we urge you to hand the entire, completed proposal to a trusted colleague who is a critical reader. If this colleague doesn't understand parts of your proposal, it is unlikely that the CO will. This individual should also check for: consistency of your discounting with the CSP chart, the commercial price list, and the GSA price list; all labor categories listed in the descriptions also having pricing and invoices; spelling; grammatical errors in past project, executive summary, and quality assurance descriptions; all solicitation requirements being answered; and sound pricing strategy. Even at EZGSA, each proposal undergoes a quality control review by an independent individual (one who did not participate in gathering and compiling the actual proposal data). We find this step integral to a high quality submission.

Remember to sign and date all required documents, including the SF1449 and checklists, as applicable.

If you are submitting your proposal in hard copy, it should be printed on the front and back of each sheet. You should mail one original and one copy and keep one copy for yourself to reference as you go through administrative review and negotiations. A few of the solicitations require that the proposals be submitted on three-hole punched paper or that you also submit a soft copy of your price list.

The address of the acquisition center to which your proposal should be submitted is within the solicitation itself as well as on the SF1449. Finally, we strongly suggest that you submit your proposal via a traceable, overnight mail service.

Chapter 3
GSA Review

3.1 Preliminary Review and Assignment of a CO

Within one or two weeks from the time your proposal arrives at the GSA acquisition center, your company's name will be entered into the GSA database. You should call the acquisition center at this time to confirm receipt of your proposal.

Soon after that, depending upon to which acquisition center your proposal has been submitted, you will either receive an email or letter with a preliminary review of your proposal or the name and contact information of your CO. If you do not receive either of these pieces of information within one month of your submission, call to ask the name of your assigned CO.

If you receive a preliminary review, it is most likely that your proposal is incomplete, does not sufficiently answer the evaluation points, or that some data in it does not match information you have provided to CCR, Dun & Bradstreet, or ORCA. If your proposal does not answer the proposed SIN's statement of work, it may be rejected outright.

Once you know the name and contact information for your CO, you should call or email the CO to introduce yourself.

3.2 Administrative and Technical Review

Within another two to four weeks, you should receive an administrative review letter from your CO. In this letter, more detailed questions about your proposal are addressed, including discrepancies between delivery dates, maximum orders, and FOB terms. S/he may request more information about past performances, customer classes and discounts, or other items. Most often, you will be required to return your answers within seven to ten days.

Your reply should be succinct and directly answer all questions, in the order they were asked. Be careful to check through your original proposal to ensure that your administrative review answers conform to information already provided. If you find that you have provided incorrect information on your original proposal, explain the mistake in your reply to the CO with the correct information.

Within one to two days of returning your reply, call or email the CO to confirm receipt.

3.3 Financial Review

Companies may be chosen to undergo an additional financial review for various reasons: some Schedules require all applicants to do so; in others, newer companies or those with questionable financial statements are sent for review; others utilize a random draw.

If your company is selected for a financial review, your CO will first complete his/her administrative review of your proposal and determine how s/he will approach negotiations. The CO then sends your financial statements to the GSA Office of the Inspector General (OIG) in Kansas City, where all such reviews are completed. Through your CO, this office asks you to complete a number of forms demonstrating your financial stability. If your company is not yet financially stable, or is going through a bit of a difficult spot, the OIG may see fit to reject your claim of fiscal competency and state that it believes you would be unable to maintain the business so that your GSA Schedule would be productive. You will be notified of the OIG's decision through your CO. You are not given access to the OIG reviewer at any time during the process, and the OIG's decision cannot be appealed.

However, if your company fits under SBA's small business size standards, you can ask SBA to issue a Certificate of Competency (COC), which will override the rejection. The COC program was formed so that a small business can appeal a determination that it is unable to fulfill the requirements of a specific government contract. From the SBA website:

> "When the small business applies for a COC, SBA industrial and financial specialists conduct a detailed review of the firm's capabilities to perform on the contract. If the business demonstrates the ability to perform, the SBA issues a COC to the CO.

“The COC program helps ensure that small businesses, especially those which are newly entering into the federal procurement arena, are given a fair opportunity to compete for and receive government contracts. [It] is carried out by a specialized SBA field staff of individuals with technical, engineering, and government procurement backgrounds in cooperation with financial specialists, also of the field organization. Upon receipt of a COC application, the SBA notifies the contracting officer of the purchasing agency that the prospective contractor has applied, and a team of financial and technical personnel surveys the firm’s potential for the specific acquisition in question. During the evaluation, SBA considers credit ratings, past performance, management capabilities, management schedules, and the prospects for obtaining needed financial help or equipment.

“The team’s findings are presented to a COC Review Committee composed of legal, technical and financial representatives, which makes a detailed review of the case and recommends approval or disapproval. If the decision is negative, the firm and the purchasing agency are so informed; if affirmative, a letter certifying the responsibility of the firm to perform the contract (the Certificate of Competency) is sent to the purchasing agency. By the terms of the Small

Business Act, the COC is conclusive on questions of responsibility, and the contract is awarded."

If rejected from Kansas City and/or the SBA, your entire proposal will be rejected. You may re-submit your proposal in a few months, but your financial information will certainly be immediately sent back to the OIG; you should therefore be prepared to demonstrate improved financial capability.

3.4 Negotiations

Once your administrative review is completed, your CO will move forward to negotiations. Some COs prefer to conduct negotiations on the phone, others through email, and a few others ask you to meet them face to face.

During negotiations, your CO will attempt to get the best value for the taxpayer. S/he will pay close attention to your CSP chart and discounting practices when determining the strategy to use. Some COs are more aggressive in negotiations than others; thus, like all negotiation scenarios, those with the GSA can be amicable or very pressured. As the vendor, you should take the time to educate yourself on your rights in negotiations and prepare well to know what concessions you are willing and able to make.

The final awarded price will serve as a ceiling selling price and government buyers may well seek additional concessions at the time of purchase. Keep this in mind when you negotiate your pricing for the base contract.

3.5 Final Proposal Revision (FPR)

The FPR is a two to three page document that your CO has in template form and uses for each of his/her contracts. In the FPR, you identify your basis of award customer (determined during negotiations). Additionally, you list changes to the proposal itself made during administrative review and concessions made during negotiations. Since the FPR is usually written with the CO's template and terms already determined, acceptance is to be expected.

However, a CO may not understand or represent all issues the way you believe was decided during review and negotiations. This can vary from time of delivery to additional discounts to FOB terms. We urge you to read the FPR closely and compare it to your copy of the administrative review reply and notes from the negotiations before placing it on your own letterhead, filling in the blanks, and signing it. Many COs ask you to fax your FPR to them and then overnight mail the original copy. Remember to always keep a copy of the document for your files.

Confirm receipt of the FPR with your CO within a few days of sending it.

3.6 Award

Soon after the FPR has been completed and accepted, your CO will give you an award number. Congratulations! You are now able to utilize that award number with purchasing and procurement officers. Your CO will send award documents to you that explain steps required of your company now that it is a GSA Schedule contract holder.

Chapter 4
Other Things to Know

4.1 Price Reduction Clause

The price reduction clause is an extremely important concept for the GSA Schedule holder. Basically, when the prices decrease or discounts increase for the class of customer upon which your contract was negotiated, you must continue to offer the same ratio of prices and/or discounts on your GSA Schedule. The government wants to continue to get a price as good as or better than your commercial customers, or your most favored commercial customers, based on similar terms, quantities, and conditions.

4.2 508 Compliance

Section 508 of 29 United States Code requires that federal agencies' electronic and information technology is accessible to people with disabilities. To learn more about your own responsibilities under Section 508, you can go to *Section 508 Compliance* at http://www.ezgsa.com/sub_links/dsp_links.shtml.

4.3 JWOD

If you are proposing to provide items such as office supplies, janitorial products, or sorbents (among others), you must ensure that the items are not already provided under the Javits-Wagner-O'Day (JWOD) Program.

Under JWOD, a wide array of products are manufactured by people who are blind or have other severe disabilities. If you propose to provide these products, you must sell JWOD-made items. You may not sell products that are identical or equivalent to JWOD items. To become a JWOD reseller or to search the JWOD list of products and services, go to the *JWOD Information* link at http://www.ezgsa.com/sub_links/dsp_links.shtml.

4.4 Marketing plan

A few of the Schedules (such as Hardware Superstore and 03FAC) require that you provide a plan for marketing your products or services to the government. This does not have to be too detailed, but should include the following points:

- ☐ How do you anticipate marketing your product or service to the federal customer?
- ☐ Do you have current federal customers who you anticipate would use your GSA Schedule contract, if awarded one?
- ☐ Have you had previous government sales? If so, summarize with the estimated value of the sales.
- ☐ Provide a list of potential federal customers in your area.
- ☐ How much of your total annual sales for the SIN(s) being offered have been to the federal government?

Conclusion

By following the directions and tips we've outlined in this guide you should be well on your way to completing a strong and well positioned GSA Schedule proposal.

The award of your contract, a major milestone to be sure, is a starting point – your fishing license, if you will – not the final goal. It is critical to have your "license," but there are more steps you must take to complete the process and maximize your chances for catching the "big fish" - your share of billions of dollars of federal sales.

As you move forward, asking yourself and your business team the following questions may help you in most effectively positioning yourself in the federal market:

Marketing and Sales:

- Have you examined the business opportunities for your company in the federal market?
- Have you developed a business strategy for pproaching the federal market?
- Have you developed a sales strategy for the federal market?
- Do you need a marketing strategy and/or campaign to brand your company for the unique federal market?
- Do you understand how Blanket Purchase Agreements and Teaming Agreements under your GSA Schedule

o your benefit?

th the time and effort for a GSA Schedule let it gather dust in the bottom drawer. Search for ...ble opportunities for business. Make your goods and services known to the government buyer. Do not rely on the government to seek you out. There is a world of trade shows, journals, newsletters, blogs, conferences, Request for Proposals/Quotes and a multitude of other innovative resources that can help make your company known.

Contract Administration:

- •Do you understand the compliance requirements of your GSA Schedule?
- •Have you tasked an individual within your organization with the responsibility of monitoring the Basis of Award and Price Reduction Clause of your GSA Schedule?
- •Do you understand how and when you may propose modifications to your contract, and that you must keep your GSA Schedule price list current?
- •Are you prepared to upload to *GSA Advantage!*?
- •Do you understand such important clauses as the Trade Agreements, open market items and contract scope?

We strongly recommend that you adopt a set
Operating Procedures for contract complian
summarize as:

Best Practices Roundup

- Monitor the **B**asis of Award
- Monitor the **P**rice List
- Monitor the **R**eporting and Registrations

We wish you the greatest success with the offer process and beyond. Please feel free to contact us with your success stories, frustrations and questions. We will always reply. You can contact us at 301/913-5000 or email your request to handbook@ezgsa.com.

Scott and *Judith*

Appendix A – GSA Schedules

00CORP THE CONSOLIDATED SCHEDULE (formerly Corporate Contracts Schedule) - Refer to each Special Item Number (SIN) for a point of contact and the individual schedule reference for additional providers of the item. Pursuant to Section 211 of the e-Gov Act of 2002, Cooperative Purchasing provides authorized State and local government entities access to information technology items offered through GSA's Schedule 70 and the Consolidated Products and Services Schedule contracts for associated special item numbers. Contracts with the COOP PURC icon indicate that authorized state and local government entities may procure from that contract.

00JWOD NIB/NISH PRODUCTS

03FAC FACILITIES MAINTENANCE AND MANAGEMENT

23 V VEHICULAR MULTIPLE AWARD SCHEDULE (VMAS)

26 I TIRES, PNEUMATIC (NEW), FOR PASSENGER, LIGHT TRUCK, MEDIUM TRUCK, AND BUS, AND RETREAD SERVICES

36 THE OFFICE, IMAGING AND DOCUMENT SOLUTION

48 TRANSPORTATION, DELIVERY AND RELOCATION SOLUTIONS

51 V HARDWARE SUPERSTORE - This includes Lawn Mowers, Tractors, Utility Vehicles, Edgers, Trimmers, Tillers, Spreaders, Sprayers, Vacuums, Sweepers, Snow Blowers and Throwers, Cattle Guards, Chain Saws, Parts and Accessories, Household and Office Appliances, Tools, Tool Kits, Tool Boxes, Woodworking and Metal

Working Machinery, Related Leasing and Rentals, Paints, Sealants, Adhesives and Lubricants

520 FINANCIAL AND BUSINESS SOLUTIONS (FABS)

541 ADVERTISING & INTEGRATED MARKETING SOLUTIONS (AIMS)

56 BUILDINGS AND BUILDING MATERIALS/INDUSTRIAL SERVICES AND SUPPLIES

58 I PROFESSIONAL AUDIO/VIDEO, TELECOMMUNICATIONS, AND SECURITY SOLUTIONS 599 TRAVEL SERVICES SOLUTIONS

621 I PROFESSIONAL AND ALLIED HEALTHCARE STAFFING SERVICES

621 II MEDICAL LABORATORY TESTING AND ANALYSIS SERVICES

621 III HOME INFUSION THERAPY SERVICES,/PSC Q999 - OTHER MEDICAL SERVICES - COMING SOON

621 V TELERADIOLOGY SERVICES - COMING SOON

65 I B PHARMACEUTICALS AND DRUGS - Please note: this schedule now contains Antiseptic Liquid Skin Cleansing Detergents and Soaps, Dispensers and Accessories.

65 II A MEDICAL EQUIPMENT AND SUPPLIES

65 II C DENTAL EQUIPMENT AND SUPPLIES

65 II F PATIENT MOBILITY DEVICES - (INCLUDING WHEELCHAIRS, SCOOTERS, WALKERS) 65 V A X-RAY EQUIPMENT AND SUPPLIES - (INCLUDING MEDICAL AND

DENTAL X-RAY FILM)

65 VII INVITRO DIAGNOSTICS, REAGENTS, TEST KITS AND TEST SETS

66 II J TEST AND MEASUREMENT EQUIPMENT, AVIATION INSTRUMENTS AND EQUIPMENT AIRCRAFT COMPONENTS, MAINTENANCE AND REPAIR SERVICES, AND UNMANNED SCIENTIFIC VEHICLES

66 II N CHEMISTRY, BIOCHEMISTRY, CLINICAL INSTRUMENTS, GENERAL PURPOSE LABORATORY INSTRUMENTS, LABORATORY FURNISHINGS AND ACCESSORIES, AND RELATED SERVICES

66 II Q GEOPHYSICAL, ENVIRONMENTAL ANALYSIS EQUIPMENT AND SERVICES - Geophysical, Environmental, Analysis & Hazard Equipment

66 III CLINICAL ANALYZERS, LABORATORY, COST-PER-TEST

67 PHOTOGRAPHIC EQUIPMENT - CAMERAS, PHOTOGRAPHIC PRINTERS AND RELATED SUPPLIES & SERVICES (DIGITAL AND FILM-BASED)

69 TRAINING AIDS & DEVICES, INSTRUCTOR-LED TRAINING; COURSE DEVELOPMENT; TEST ADMINISTRATION - Programmed learning devices

70 GENERAL PURPOSE COMMERCIAL INFORMATION TECHNOLOGY EQUIPMENT, SOFTWARE, AND SERVICES - Pursuant to Section 211 of the e-Gov Act of 2002, Cooperative Purchasing provides authorized State and local government entities access to information technology items offered through GSA's Schedule 70 and the Corporate contracts for associated special item numbers. Contracts with the COOP PURC icon indicate that authorized state and local government entities may procure from that contract.

71 I OFFICE FURNITURE

71 II HOUSEHOLD AND QUARTERS FURNITURE

71 II H PACKAGED FURNITURE

71 II K COMPREHENSIVE FURNITURE MANAGEMENT SERVICES (CFMS)

71 III SPECIAL USE FURNITURE - Preschool and Classroom, Auditorium and Theater Seating; Library-Wood, Metal or Plastic Furniture; Storage Cabinets for Forms and Flammable Liquids Card-Size Filing Cabinets; Mail Sorting and Distribution Bins, Racks and Carts; Light-Duty Small Parts Cabinets; and Plastic Storage Bins; Hospital Patient Room Furniture; Cafeteria and Food Service; Drafting Stools, Clothing Lockers and Locker Benches; Workbenches, Worktables and High - Density Storage Cabinets and Enclosure Systems for Modular Electronic Equipment

71 III E MISCELLANEOUS FURNITURE - Security Filing Cabinets, Safes, Vault Doors, Map And Plan Files And Accessories, Comsec Containers And Special Access Control Containers

72 I A FLOOR COVERINGS - Carpet, Rugs, Carpet Tiles And Carpet Cushions

72 II FURNISHINGS 73 FOOD SERVICE, HOSPITALITY, CLEANING EQUIPMENT AND SUPPLIES, CHEMICALS AND

SERVICES - Food Service Equipment, Supplies, and Services

736 TEMPORARY ADMINISTRATIVE AND PROFESSIONAL STAFFING (TAPS) - Temporary Administrative and Professional Staffing Services

738 II LANGUAGE SERVICES

738 X HUMAN RESOURCES & EQUAL EMPLOYMENT OPPORTUNITY SERVICES

75 OFFICE PRODUCTS/SUPPLIES AND SERVICES AND NEW PRODUCTS/TECHNOLOGY - Schedule 75 now includes Videotapes, Audiotapes, Tape Cartridges, Diskettes/Optical Disks, Disk Packs, Disk Cartridges, Anti-Glare Screens, Cleaning Equipment & Supplies, Ergonomic Devices, Next Day Desktop Delivery of Office Supplies, and Restroom Products such as Roll Toilet Tissue Dispensers, Toilet Tissue, Paper Towels, Toilet Seat Covers, Facial Tissues, and Soaps for Restroom Dispensers.

751 LEASING OF AUTOMOBILES AND LIGHT TRUCKS

76 PUBLICATION MEDIA

78 SPORTS, PROMOTIONAL, OUTDOOR, RECREATION, TROPHIES AND SIGNS (SPORTS) - Trophies, Awards, Presentations, Promotional Products, Briefcases and Carrying Cases, Trade Show Displays & Exhibit Systems And All Related Products

81 I B SHIPPING, PACKAGING AND PACKING SUPPLIES - Bags, Sacks, Cartons, Crates, Packaging And Packing Bulk Material

84 TOTAL SOLUTIONS FOR LAW ENFORCEMENT, SECURITY, FACILITIES MANAGEMENT, FIRE, RESCUE, CLOTHING, MARINE CRAFT AND EMERGENCY/DISASTER RESPONS -

Marine Craft and Equipment

871 PROFESSIONAL ENGINEERING SERVICES

871 II ENERGY SERVICES

873 LABORATORY TESTING AND ANALYSIS SERVICES

874 MISSION ORIENTED BUSINESS INTEGRATED SERVICES (MOBIS)

874 V LOGISTICS WORLDWIDE (LOGWORLD)

899 ENVIRONMENTAL SERVICES

Appendix B
GSA Schedules Sales Report

All Schedules by Fiscal Year – FY2005

Total Sales $33,571,112,107.00

Schedule	Sales Amount	Schedule	Sales Amount
CORP	$986,351,990.00	72 I A	$42,376,977.00
JWOD	$10,670,286.00	72 II	$20,107,947.00
23 V	$172,482,908.00	73	$181,584,627.00
26 I	$16,065,885.00	75	$555,942,252.00
36	$756,047,161.00	76	$87,347,919.00
03FAC	$61,330,360.00	78	$393,659,782.00
48	$404,735,559.00	81 I B	$89,720,578.00
51 V	$589,196,188.00	84	$2,272,328,739.00
56	$526,141,223.00	421 I A	$13,740.00
58 I	$200,922,725.00	520	$767,115,666.00
58 V A	$0.00	541	$351,769,598.00
66 II J	$261,547,330.00	599	$81,355,231.00
66 II N	$261,187,751.00	736	$113,223,947.00
66 II Q	$70,129,428.00	738 I	$77,750.00
67	$36,709,157.00	738 II	$120,922,933.00
69	$148,701,070.00	738 X	$137,798,203.00
70	$16,535,505,632.00	751	$10,056,339.00
71 I	$862,645,258.00	871	$2,298,812,449.00
71 II	$90,378,211.00	871 II	$42,580,412.00
71 II H	$99,024,067.00	873	$26,864,293.00

Schedule	Sales Amount	Schedule	Sales Amount
71 II K	$29,794,346.00	874	$2,926,382,127.00
71 III	$80,203,758.00	874 V	$441,753,608.00
71 III E	$28,553,657.00	899	$380,993,040.00

All Schedules by Fiscal Year – FY2004

Total Sales $31,866,718,551

Schedule	Sales Amount	Schedule	Sales Amount
CORP	$986,351,990.00	72 I A	$42,376,977.00
JWOD	$10,670,286.00	72 II	$20,107,947.00
23 V	$172,482,908.00	73	$181,584,627.00
26 I	$16,065,885.00	75	$555,942,252.00
36	$756,047,161.00	76	$87,347,919.00
03FAC	$61,330,360.00	78	$393,659,782.00
48	$404,735,559.00	81 I B	$89,720,578.00
51 V	$589,196,188.00	84	$2,272,328,739.00
56	$526,141,223.00	421 I A	$13,740.00
58 I	$200,922,725.00	520	$767,115,666.00
58 V A	$0.00	541	$351,769,598.00
66 II J	$261,547,330.00	599	$81,355,231.00
66 II N	$261,187,751.00	736	$113,223,947.00
66 II Q	$70,129,428.00	738 I	$77,750.00
67	$36,709,157.00	738 II	$120,922,933.00
69	$148,701,070.00	738 X	$137,798,203.00
70	$16,535,505,632.00	751	$10,056,339.00
71 I	$862,645,258.00	871	$2,298,812,449.00
71 II	$90,378,211.00	871 II	$42,580,412.00

Schedule	Sales Amount	Schedule	Sales Amount
71 II H	$99,024,067.00	873	$26,864,293.00
71 II K	$29,794,346.00	874	$2,926,382,127.00
71 III	$80,203,758.00	874 V	$441,753,608.00
71 III E	$28,553,657.00	899	$380,993,040.00

* Source : GSA, September 2005

Appendix C
Common Acronyms

Note: Some of the more common acronyms you may run into during a GSA schedule proposal effort are in bold.

A

ACO ....Administrative Contracting Officer

ADR..............................Alternate Dispute Resolution

ADPE ....Automatic Data Processing Equipment

ANSI............................American National Standards Institute

B

BA.................................Basic Agreement

BAFO ....Best and Final Offer

BOA..............................Basic Ordering Agreement

BPA..............................Blanket Purchase Agreement

C

CA.................................Competition Advocate

CBD..............................Commerce Business Daily

CFR..............................Code of Federal Regulations

CICA............................Competition In Contracting Act

CIO ....Chief Information Officer

CIM..............................Corporate Information Management

CLIN............................Contract Line Item Number

CO ....Contracting Officer

CONUS.......................Continental United States (includes the 48 contiguous United States plus District of Columbia)

COR..............................Contracting Officer's Representative

COTR............................Contracting Officer's Technical Representative

COTS...........................Commercial Off The Shelf

CPAF.............................Cost Plus Award Fee

CPFF.............................Cost Plus Fixed Fee

CPIF..............................Cost Plus Incentive Fee

CSP...............................Commercial Sales Practice

D

D&F..............................Determinations and Findings

DCAA...........................Defense Contract Audit Agency

DFAR............................Defense Federal Acquisition

DO................................Delivery Order

DOD.............................Department of Defense

DSO..............................Designated Senior Official

E

EBBS............................Electronic Bulletin Board System

EC.................................Electronic Commerce

ECP..............................Engineering Change Proposal

EDI...............................Electronic Data Interchange

EFOIA..........................Electronic Freedom Of Information Act

F

FAC..............................Federal Acquisition Circular

FACNET.......................Federal Acquisition Computer Network

FAR..............................Federal Acquisition Regulation

FARA............................Federal Acquisition Reform Act

FASA............................Federal Acquisition Streamlining Act

F&D..............................Finding and Determinations

FED-STD.....................Federal Standard

FFP..............................Firm Fixed Price

FIPS ....Federal Information Processing Standard

FMSS............................Financial Management Systems Software

FOB..............................Free On Board

FOIA.............................Freedom Of Information Act

FEDC............................Federal Equipment Data Center

FPDC............................Federal Procurement Data Center

FPR ....Final Proposal Revision

FPOC............................Fixed Price Options Clause

FSS ....Federal Supply Schedule

FTR..............................Federal Travel Regulations

G

GAO............................General Accounting Office

GFE..............................Government Furnished Equipment

GOCO...........................Government Owned Contractor Operated

GOSIP...........................Government Open System Interconnection Profile

GPO ....Government Printing Office

GPRA ....Government Performance and Results Act

GSA..............................General Services Administration

GWAC ....Government wide Acquisition Contract

H

HPA...............................Head of Procuring Activity

I

IDDQ............................Indefinite Delivery – Definite Quantity

IDIQ............................Indefinite Delivery – Indefinite Quantity

IG ....Inspector General

IRM................................Information Resource Management

IT ....Information Technology

ITMRA.........................Information Technology Management Reform Act

J

JOFOC..........................Justification For Other Than Full & Open Competition

JTR................................Joint Travel Regulations

L

LCC ....Life Cycle Cost

LOI................................Letter of Intent

LTD...............................Live Test Demonstration

LTOP.............................Lease to Ownership Plan

LWOP...........................Lease with Option to Purchase

M

MAS ....Multiple Award Schedule

MIL-STD.....................Military Standard

MIPR ....Military Interdepartmental Purchase Request

MOT ....Maximum Order Threshold

N

NAICS..........................

NIST ....National Institute of Standards

NPR ....National Performance Review

O

OCD..............................Operational Capability Demonstration

OCONUS ....Outside Continental United States (includes AK, HI and territories of the United States)

OFPP.............................Office of Federal Procurement Policy

OIRM ....Office of Information Resource Management
OMB.............................Office of Management and Budget
O&M ....Operation and Maintenance

P

PASS.............................Procurement Automated Source System
PCO ....Procuring Contracting Officer
P&CV............................Performance and Capability Validation
PI...................................Procurement Integrity
PM ....Program Manager
PO.................................Purchase Order
PPCC ....Past Performance Comparison Chart
PPI ....Past Performance Information
PPM..............................Principal Period of Maintenance
PRRA............................Paperwork Reduction Reauthorization Act
PV ....Present Value

Q

QA ....Quality Assurance
QBL..............................Qualified Bidders List
QC ....Quality Control
QML ....Qualified Manufacturers List
QPL...............................Qualified Products List

R

RFC...............................Request for Comment
RFI................................Request for Information
RFP...............................Request for Proposal
RFQ ....Request for Quotation
RV ....Residual Value

S

SADBU ....Small & Disadvantaged Business Utilization

SADBUS......................Small & Disadvantaged Business Utilization Specialist

SAP................................Simplified Acquisition Procedure

SAT ....Simplified Acquisition Threshold

SBA................................Small Business Administration

SCF ....Simplified Contract Format

SDB ....Small Disadvantaged Business

SIC.................................Standard Industrial Classification

SIN.................................Special Item Number

SOW.............................Statement of Work

SSA................................Source Selection Authority or Social Security Administration (content sensitive)

SSEB ....Source Selection Evaluation Board

SSP................................Source Selection Plan

T

Ts&Cs ....Term and Conditions

T&M............................Time and materials

TM ....Task Monitor

TO..................................Task Order

TCO ....Termination Contracting Officer

TEP ....Technical Evaluation Panel

T for C ....Termination for Convenience

T for D ....Termination for Default

TIN ....Taxpayer Identification Number

TINA.............................Truth in Negotiations Act

TPR...............................Temporary Price Reduction

U

UCF .... Uniform Contract Format

V

VAN .... Value Added Network

VAR .... Value Added Reseller

Appendix D - CCR Handbook

(The information in this appendix can also be downloaded from http://www.ccr.gov/handbook.asp.)

Introduction

The Central Contractor Registration (CCR) is the primary vendor database for the U.S. Federal Government. The CCR collects, validates, stores and disseminates data in support of agency acquisition missions.

Both current and potential government vendors are required to register in CCR in order to do be awarded contracts by the government. Vendors are required to complete a one-time registration to provide basic information relevant to procurement and financial transactions. Vendors must update or renew their registration annually to maintain an active status.

CCR validates the vendor's information and electronically shares the secure and encrypted data with the federal agencies' finance offices to facilitate paperless payments through electronic funds transfer (EFT). Additionally, CCR shares the data with government procurement and electronic business systems.

Please note that any information provided in your registration may be shared with authorized government offices. Registration does not, however, guarantee business with the government.

Who registers in CCR?

- According to the FAR 4.1102 (October 1, 2003), "Prospective contractors shall be registered in the CCR database prior to award of a contract or agreement"

For registration assistance, contact the Procurement Technical Assistance Center (PTAC), http://www.dla.mil/db, or the Small Business Administration (SBA) office in your area.

If you have further questions regarding this letter please call the CCR Assistance Center at 1-888-227-2423.

Appendix E – FIPS PUB 161-2

Federal Information
Processing Standards Publication 161-2

1996 April 29
Announcing the Standard for

ELECTRONIC DATA INTERCHANGE (EDI)

(The Foreword, Abstract, and Key Words can be found at the end of this document.)

Federal Information Processing Standards Publications (FIPS PUBS) are issued by the National Institute of Standards and Technology after approval by the Secretary of Commerce pursuant to Section 111(d) of the Federal Property and Administrative Services Act of 1949, as amended by the Computer Security Act of 1987, Public Law 100-235.

1. Name of Standard. Electronic Data Interchange (EDI) (FIPS PUB 161-2).

2. Category of Standard. Electronic Data Interchange.

3. Explanation.

3.1. Definition and Use of EDI. EDI is the computer-to-computer interchange of strictly formatted messages that represent documents other than monetary instruments. EDI implies a sequence of messages between two parties, either of whom may serve as originator or recipient. The formatted data representing the documents may be transmitted from originator to recipient via telecommunications or physically transported on electronic storage media.

In EDI, the usual processing of received messages is by computer only. Human intervention in the processing of a received message is typically intended only for error conditions, for quality review, and for special situations. For example, the transmission of binary or textual data is not EDI as defined here unless the data are treated as one or more data elements of an EDI message and are not normally intended for human interpretation as part of on-line data processing.

An example of EDI is a set of interchanges between a buyer and a seller. Messages from buyer to seller could include, for example, request for quotation (RFQ), purchase order, receiving advice and payment advice; messages from seller to buyer could include, similarly, bid in response to RFQ, purchase order acknowledgment, shipping notice and invoice. These messages may simply provide information, e.g., receiving advice or shipping notice, or they may include data that may be interpreted as a legally binding obligation, e.g., bid in response to RFQ or purchase order.

EDI is being used also for an increasingly diverse set of concerns, for example, for interchanges between healthcare providers and insurers, for travel and hotel bookings, for education administration, and for government regulatory, statistical and tax reporting.

3.2. Standards Required for EDI. From the point of view of the standards needed, EDI may be defined as an interchange between computers of a sequence of standardized messages taken from a predetermined set of message types. Each message is composed, according to a standardized syntax, of a sequence of standardized data elements. It is the standardization of message formats using a standard syntax, and the standardization of data elements within the messages, that makes possible the assembling, disassembling, and processing of the messages by computer.

Implementation of EDI requires the use of a family of interrelated standards. Standards are required for, at minimum: (a) the syntax used to compose the messages and separate the various parts of a message, (b) types and definitions of application data elements, most of variable length, (c) the message types, defined by the identification and sequence of data elements forming each message, and (d) the definitions and sequence of control data elements in message headers and trailers.

Additional standards may define: (e) a set of short sequences of data elements called data segments, (f) the manner in which more than one message may be included in a single transmission, and (g) the manner of adding protective measures for integrity, confidentiality, and authentication into transmitted messages.

3.3. Limited Coverage of this Standard. This FIPS covers only EDI. It does not cover other forms of electronic interchange, for example, systems of interchange that do not consist of messages taken from a predetermined set. Additionally, an interchange application including only one or two predetermined message types using only fixed-length data elements is excluded from coverage of this FIPS. This FIPS also is not intended to cover transmissions from medical, laboratory, or environment-sensing instrumentation.

3.4. The Long-Range Goal for EDI Standards. There are several different EDI standards in use today, but the achievement of a single universally-used family of EDI standards is a long-range goal. A single universally-used family of standards would make use of EDI more efficient and minimize aggregate costs of use. Specifically, it would (a) minimize needs for training of personnel in use and maintenance of EDI standards, (b) eliminate duplication of functionality and the costs of achieving that duplication now existing in different systems of standards, (c) minimize requirements for different kinds of translation software, and (d) allow for a universal set of data elements that would ease the flow of data among different but interconnected applications, and thereby maximize useful information interchange.

This FIPS PUB recognizes the reality that some families of EDI standards were developed to provide solutions to immediate needs, and that inclusion of the goal of universality in their development would have unacceptably delayed their availability. However, a future is envisioned in which the benefits of universality outweigh the sunk costs in specialized solutions, leading first to cooperation among standards developers, then to harmonization of standards, and eventually to a single universally accepted family of EDI standards.

3.5. Adoption of Specific Families of Standards. This FIPS PUB adopts, with specific conditions specified below, the families of EDI standards known as X12, UN/EDIFACT and HL7. This FIPS PUB does not mandate the implementation of EDI systems within the Federal Government; rather it requires the use of the identified families of standards with specified constraints when Federal departments or agencies implement EDI systems.

The UN/EDIFACT standards may be used for any application, domestic or international. The X12 standards may be used for any domestic application. The HL7 standards are adopted as an alternative for certain healthcare applications, specifically for transmission of patient records and of clinical, epidemiological, and regulatory data. HL7 standards are not to be used for healthcare insurance administrative applications, such as for enrollments, claims, and claim payments, or for any aspect of the Government procurement cycle, such as for registration of vendors, RFQ, purchase order, shipping notice, or payment advice.

The cross-use of data elements is encouraged. A data element received through one system of EDI standards, or through a non-

EDI interchange, may be re-transmitted as a data element in any of the approved systems of EDI standards.

The adopted standards were developed by the following organizations: the X12 standards by Accredited Standards Committee X12 on Electronic Data Interchange (ASC X12), accredited by the American National Standards Institute (ANSI); the HL7 standards by Health Level Seven, Inc., an ANSI-accredited standards developer; and the UN/EDIFACT standards by the United Nations (UN) Economic Commission for Europe - Working Party (Four) on Facilitation of International Trade Procedures (UN/ECE/WP.4). Technical input from the United States in the development of UN/EDIFACT at the UN is through the Pan American EDIFACT Board (PAEB). The PAEB is separate from ASC X12, and it serves as the coordinating body for national standards organizations of North, Central, and South America.

3.6. Status of this FIPS PUB Revision. FIPS PUB 161-2 supersedes FIPS PUB 161-1 in its entirety. FIPS PUB 161-2 contains editorial changes, updated references to documents and organizations, and new guidance to agencies on the selection of national and international standards and implementation conventions. This guidance is based on recent voluntary industry standards activities and on the Federal Government initiative that commenced with the Presidential Memorandum of October 26, 1993 entitled "Streamlining Procurement Through Electronic Commerce."

4. Approving Authority. Secretary of Commerce.

5. Maintenance Agency. U.S. Department of Commerce, National Institute of Standards and Technology (NIST), Computer Systems Laboratory.

6. Cross Index and Related Documents.

6.1. Cross Index.

- \- FIPS PUB 146-2, Profiles for Open Systems Internetworking Technologies, May 1995.

6.2. Related Documents.

- \- ASC X12W/95-137, The ASC X12 Plan for Technical Migration to and Administrative Alignment With UN/EDIFACT (amended), 5/8/95.

- \- NIST Special Publication 500-224, Stable Implementation Agreements for Open System Environment, Version 8, Edition 1, 12/94.

- \- NIST Special Publication 800-9, Good Security Practices for Electronic Commerce, Including Electronic Data Interchange, 12/93.

- \- Office of Management and Budget (OMB) Circular A-119 (revised), Federal Participation in the Development and Use of Voluntary Standards, 10/93.

- \- UN/ECE/WP.4 - Recommendation No. 25 on the Use of the UN/ EDIFACT Standard, 9/95.

6.3. Sources of Documents. For the source of cited NIST publications, including FIPS PUBS, see Section 13. For the source of X12, UN/EDIFACT and HL7 documents, see Subsection 10.1.

7. Objectives. The primary objectives of this standard are:

a. to ease the interchange of data sent electronically by use of common standards that allow for automated message processing;
b. to promote the achievement of the benefits of EDI: reduced paperwork, fewer transcription errors, faster response time for procurement and customer needs, reduced inventory requirements, more timely payment of vendors, and closer coordination of data

being processed on different computers for the same application;
c. to promote migration to a universally used family of EDI standards, in order to further Government efficiency and to minimize the cost of EDI implementation by preventing duplication of effort.

8. Applicability.

8.1. Conditions of Application. EDI may be employed with any type of operational data representable as a sequence of data elements that is needed to be transmitted or received on a repetitive basis by a Federal agency in the course of its activities. This standard is applicable to the interchange of such data on a particular subject within a Federal agency, or between a Federal agency and another organization (which may be another Federal agency), if (1) the data are to be transmitted electronically or physically transported between computers using EDI, and (2) the necessary standard messages meeting the data requirements of the Federal agency for the subject of the interchange have been developed and approved, and are acceptable for use under the conditions set forth in this FIPS PUB.

8.2. Subject Matter. Examples of applications (not necessarily the subject of current standards) are:

a. vendor search and selection: price/sales catalogs, bids, proposals, requests for quotations, notices of contract solicitation, debarment data, trading partner profiles;
b. contract award: notices of award, purchase orders, purchase order acknowledgments, purchase order changes;
c. product data: specifications, manufacturing instructions, reports of test results, safety data;
d. shipping, forwarding, and receiving: shipping manifests, bills of lading, shipping status reports, receiving reports;
e. customs: release information; manifest update;
f. payment information: invoices, remittance advices, payment status inquiries, payment acknowledgments;

g. inventory control: stock level reports, resupply requests, warehouse activity reports;
h. maintenance: service schedules and activity, warranty data;
i. tax-related data: tax information and filings;
j. insurance-related data: health care claim; mortgage insurance application;
k. other government activities: communications license application; court conviction record; hazardous material report; healthcare event report.

9. Coordination of Federal EDI Standards Development and Implementation.

9.1. Federal EDI Standards Management Coordinating Committee. There is established a Federal EDI Standards Management Coordinating Committee (FESMCC). The FESMCC is established to support the goal of a single face for the Federal Government to its trading partners in the use of EDI.

9.1.1. A responsibility of the FESMCC is the selection of implementation conventions (ICs) to be used with EDI interchanges between the Federal Government and its trading partners. EDI messages (also called transaction sets) are approved by standards committees with allowances for format options, in order to widen the applicability of the standards to different uses. The purpose of ICs is to select specific options in EDI standards so that interchanges are completely determined in format in advance of use.

9.1.2. The basic functions of the FESMCC are:

(a) to adopt Government-wide ICs for use with EDI standards; the goal is adoption of one IC for each functional application of a message or transaction set within a given version/release of an EDI standard;
(b) to coordinate Federal agency participation in EDI standards bodies, to assure adequate consideration of the Government's business needs and to assure consistency of position; and

(c) to share EDI information among agencies regarding current or planned implementations to avoid duplicate efforts and streamline the process.

9.1.3. Voting membership in the FESMCC shall consist of, at minimum, one representative from each participating Federal Executive Branch department and independent agency using or planning to use EDI, plus a representative from NIST. The FESMCC, under its charter and operating rules (see Subsection 9.1.5), may add additional voting representatives, including those from the other branches of the Federal Government. The chair of the FESMCC shall be elected by its membership and approved by OMB.

9.1.4. The FESMCC shall establish a secretariat in order to maintain an official registry of approved and draft ICs, provide controlled access to the registry including electronic remote access capability, provide a point of contact for publicizing draft ICs and receiving comments on them, provide a single point for submission of work requests to standards bodies, and for related functions.

9.1.5. The FESMCC shall establish a charter and operating rules to assist it in carrying out its identified functions.

9.2. Functional Work Groups

9.2.1. The FESMCC may establish Functional Work Groups (FWGs) to consider and recommend ICs in subject areas. Examples of subject areas are procurement, finance, logistics, and healthcare. Requirements for voting membership shall be established by the FESMCC under its charter and operating rules. The voting members shall elect a chair.

9.2.2. Each FWG shall recommend, to the full FESMCC, ICs that it has developed and approved as meeting Federal Government and trading partner business requirements. FWGs should consult with appropriate industry groups in the development of ICs.

9.3. Agency Responsibilities

9.3.1. Agencies shall register ICs that they are using with the FESMCC secretariat.

9.3.2. Agencies using X12, UN/EDIFACT, or HL7 versions and releases for which ICs have been established by the FESMCC shall adopt those ICs. If an IC does not meet business needs, requirements shall be submitted to the FESMCC. ICs shall be classified as Implementer's Agreements pursuant to this FIPS PUB, but are not themselves FIPS PUBs.

9.3.3. Agencies using or planning to use EDI shall designate representatives to the FESMCC and each relevant FWG.

9.3.4. Agencies requiring new EDI standards or changes to existing EDI standards to meet their business needs shall submit their requirements to the appropriate standards bodies and shall simultaneously submit their requirements to the FESMCC and relevant FWGs for coordination. Procedures and forms for submission of new requirements through ASC X12 are specified in Standing Document (SD) 2, Operations Manual, and SD6, Operations Manual for UN/EDIFACT Standards. These manuals are available from Data Interchange Standards Association, Inc. (DISA, Inc.). Procedures and forms for submission of new requirements for UN/EDIFACT standards directly through the PAEB are also available from DISA, Inc. HL7 operating procedures are specified in its bylaws, available from Health Level Seven, Inc.

10. Specifications. Documents are available that define the X12, UN/EDIFACT, and HL7 standards and provide information about the standards organizations and their standards development processes. Developments are continuing in each of these families of standards.

10.1. Source of Documents. Documents concerning both the X12 and UN/EDIFACT families of standards are available from DISA, Inc. or from its named contractor. DISA, Inc. serves as the secretariat for ASC X12 and the PAEB and may be contacted at:

Data Interchange Standards Association, Inc.
1800 Diagonal Road - Suite 200
Alexandria, VA 22314-2852
Phone: (703) 548-7005

A list of available standards publications, as well as descriptive material, prices and ordering procedures, may be found in the most recent DISA, Inc. Publications Catalog.

HL7 documents are available from:

Health Level Seven, Inc.
3300 Washtenaw Avenue, Suite 227
Ann Arbor, MI 48104
Phone: (313) 677-7777

10.2. ASC X12 Documents. X12 standards are published periodically with revisions and updates, and standards included in a publication may have one of two possible statuses:

(1) Draft Standards for Trial Use (DSTUs); these are fully approved by ASC X12, and are typically published as "releases" at one-year intervals. DSTU Version 3, Release 4, identified as 003040, was published in 12/93; Version 3, Release 5, identified as 003050, was published in 12/94. The next release, identified as 003060, is available as of 1/96.
(2) American National Standards (ANSs); these are fully approved by ASC X12 and by ANSI, and are typically published as "versions" at intervals of three to five years. ANS Version 3, 3/92, is functionally equivalent to DSTU Version 2, Release 4. It is expected that ANS Version 4, planned for 1997, will be functionally equivalent to DSTU Version 3, Release 7, identified as

003070.

10.3 UN/EDIFACT Documents. UN/EDIFACT standards are published periodically with revisions and updates, and standards included in a publication may have one of two possible statuses:

(1) Status 1, approved for trial use. A set of documents identified as UN/EDIFACT Draft Messages and Directories, Version D.95A, was published in 5/95. This document also included Status 2 messages. A new set of standards, identified as D.95B and also including Status 2 messages, was approved in 9/95.

(2) Status 2, fully approved by UN/ECE/WP.4. The set of Status 2 documents may be referred to as the UN Trade Data Interchange Directory (UNTDID). The last published version of Status 2 standards only, S.93A, was issued in 5/94. See also Subsection 11.4 for additional information on UN/EDIFACT Status 2.

10.4 HL7 Documents. HL7 standards are published as a single volume. The current set is Version 2.2, published 12/94. A new Version 2.3 is planned for Fall 1996. HL7 standards also have one of two possible statuses:

(1) HL7 standards, approved by the membership of HL7 but not yet approved by ANSI.

(2) American National Standards (ANSs); these are fully approved by HL7 and by ANSI.

11. Implementation.

11.1. Schedule for Adoption. FIPS PUB 161 was effective on September 30, 1991. Federal agencies that are not using EDI for subject matter for which X12, UN/EDIFACT, and HL7 standards have been approved and issued shall utilize only those standards in EDI systems that they procure or develop, subject to the qualifications of Subsections 3.5, 11.3, 11.4 and 11.5. Agencies that are using those standards shall continue to do so, subject to the same qualifications. Agencies that were using other standards on or after September 30, 1991 shall be governed by Subsection 11.6.

11.2. Acceptance of UN/EDIFACT by ASC X12. In January 1995,

ASC X12, by a membership vote, approved the ASC X12 Plan For Technical Migration To And Administrative Alignment With UN/EDIFACT. This plan was modified at the February 1995 plenary meeting of ASC X12. Key features of the modified Alignment Plan are:

(1) Draft standards based on X12 syntax or on UN/EDIFACT syntax may be submitted by ASC X12 to ANSI for processing as ANSs.
(2) X12 Release 003070 shall form the basis of Version 4 of draft proposed X12 American National Standards (ANSs).
(3) After the release of Version 4, ASC X12 shall continue for a period of time, in accordance with the plan, to develop, maintain, approve and publish X12-syntax transaction sets and supporting documents.
(4) An ASC X12 ballot shall be conducted in 1998 to determine if X12-syntax transaction set development should be terminated. If the ballot for termination is not approved, a three-year repeating cycle shall occur thereafter, until no new X12-syntax transaction sets are being developed.
11.3. Selection of a Family of Standards.

11.3.1. Different families of EDI standards are distinct, although performing similar functions; the existence of one does not preclude the others. Equivalent functionality may be obtained in any system by the addition, if required, of new or revised message formats and data elements. Software that assembles and disassembles messages and transaction sets, called translation software, is widely available, often for more than one system in the same package. In selecting a family of standards for domestic applications, agencies should attempt to maximize Government economy and efficiency and to minimize the costs imposed on U.S. businesses.

11.3.2. For any domestic application with a non-Government partner, and for related intra-Government applications, selection of a family of standards shall take into account the prevailing family used in the industry of the interchange partners for the application. However, UN/EDIFACT standards shall be employed for new or significantly upgraded interchanges in the absence of demonstrably higher costs, or at the request of interchange partners providing a significant fraction of interchange traffic. Continued long-term use and maintenance of more than one family of standards is unacceptably inefficient.

11.3.3. For international applications except as specified in Subsection 11.3.4, planning for migration to the UN/EDIFACT family of standards shall commence at this time if that family is not currently being used. A timetable for conversion to UN/ EDIFACT of existing international implementations shall be set as applicable standards and software become available. New or signifcantly upgraded interchanges shall employ only standards using UN/ EDIFACT.

11.3.4. The HL7 family of standards may be used for international applications in the fields of public health and health regulatory information, pursuant to agreements of international organizations whose membership includes representation of national or multi-national governmental health agencies. However, users shall coordinate with the developers of UN/EDIFACT, in order to prevent duplication of effort, provide for cross-use of data elements, and provide a path for harmonization and eventual migration or coalescence.

11.4. Use of Category (1) Standards. UN/EDIFACT Status 1 standards, X12 DSTUs, and HL7 standards not yet approved by ANSI are defined as Category (1) standards. UN/EDIFACT Status 2 standards and ANSs submitted by ASC X12 and HL7 are defined as Category (2) standards. Federal agencies shall use only Category (1) or Category (2) standards for EDI implementations. Industry practice is to use Category (1) standards; these represent the latest consensus and are available sooner than the corresponding full standards of Category (2). Consequently, Category (1) standards are preferred, but not mandated at this time. Note: there is a possibility that UN/EDIFACT Status 2 standards will be eliminated by UN/ECE/WP.4. In that case, UN/EDIFACT Status 1 standards would be required when UN/EDIFACT is implemented.

11.5. Continued Use of Existing Approved Implementations. An existing implementation of any version of an approved standard specified in Subsections 3.5, 11.3 and 11.4 may continue to be used as long as it continues to meet the business needs of the using agency and its interchange partners. Significant upgrades of existing implementations shall be to versions and releases for which ICs have been approved by the FESMCC, if any are available.

11.6. Continued Use of Other EDI Standards. Under the initial issue of this FIPS, Federal agencies using "industry-specific" EDI standards were permitted to use those standards for five years from September 30, 1991, i.e., until September 30, 1996. Agencies were permitted to use "industry-specific" EDI standards beyond five years only if no equivalent X12 or UN/EDIFACT standards, as appropriate, were approved and issued by September 30, 1995. If an equivalent and appropriate standard were issued after the latter date, agencies were given one year to convert. These provisions remain in effect for all application areas except healthcare.

For healthcare applications, agencies may use EDI standards other than UN/EDIFACT, X12, or HL7 through September 30, 1997. Other standards may be used beyond that date only if no functionally equivalent standards that meet the conditions of use specified in Subsections 3.5, 11.3 and 11.4 are approved and issued by September 30, 1996. If a Category (1) standard meeting business requirements and allowable conditions of use is first issued after the latter date, agencies have one year to convert following the issuance of the release containing the implementable standard.

Requirements for submission of proposed new or revised standards are specified in Subsection 9.3.4.

11.7. Security and Authentication. Agencies shall employ risk management techniques to determine the appropriate mix of security controls needed to protect specific data and systems. The selection of controls shall take into account procedures required under applicable laws and regulations.

Optional tools and techniques for implementation of security and authentication may be provided by ASC X12 and UN/ECE/WP.4 for use in connection with their respective families of standards. Agencies may utilize these tools and techniques, and/or they may utilize other methods in systems supporting the EDI data interchange. Methods and procedures implemented shall be consistent with applicable FIPS PUBS and guidance documents issued by NIST.

12. Waivers. Under certain exceptional circumstances, the heads of Federal departments and agencies may approve waivers to Federal Information Processing Standards (FIPS). The head of such agency may redelegate such authority only to a senior official designated pursuant to Section 3506(a) of Title 44, U.S. Code.

Waivers shall be granted only when:

a. Compliance with a standard would adversely affect the accomplishment of the mission of an operator of a Federal computer system, or
b. Cause a major adverse financial impact on the operator which is not offset by Government-wide savings.
Agency heads may act upon a written waiver request containing the information detailed above. Agency heads may also act without a written waiver request when they determine that conditions for meeting the standard cannot be met. Agency heads may approve waivers only by a written decision which explains the basis on which the agency head made the required finding(s). A copy

of each such decision, with procurement sensitive or classified portions clearly identified, shall be sent to: National Institute of Standards and Technology; Attn: FIPS Waiver Decisions, Technology Building, Room B-154; Gaithersburg, MD 20899.

In addition, notice of each waiver granted and each delegation of authority to approve waivers shall be sent promptly to the Committee on Government Reform and Oversight of the House of Representatives and the Committee on Governmental Affairs of the Senate and shall be published promptly in the Federal Register.

When the determination on a waiver applies to the procurement of equipment and/or services, a notice of the waiver determination must be published in the Commerce Business Daily as part of the notice of solicitation for offers of an acquisition or, if the waiver determination is made after that notice is published, by amendment to such notice.

A copy of the waiver, any supporting documents, the document approving the waiver and any supporting and accompanying documents, with such deletions as the agency is authorized and decides to make under 5 U.S.C. Sec. 552(b), shall be part of the procurement documentation and retained by the agency.

13. Where to Obtain Copies of NIST Publications. Copies of this publication and NIST publications referenced in Section 6 are for sale by the National Technical Information Service (NTIS), U.S. Department of Commerce, Springfield, VA 22161; phone (703) 487- 4650. When ordering this publication, refer to Federal Information Processing Standards Publication 161-2 (FIPSPUB161-2), and title. Payment may be made by check, money order, or NTIS deposit account.

Appendix F - FAR 2.101, Micro-Purchase Threshold

"Micro-purchase" means an acquisition of supplies or services, the aggregate amount of which does not exceed the micro-purchase threshold.

"Micro-purchase threshold" means $2,500, except it means—

(1) For construction subject to the Davis-Bacon Act, $2,000; and

(2) For acquisitions of supplies or services that, as determined by the head of the agency, are to be used to support a contingency operation or to facilitate defense against or recovery from nuclear, biological, chemical or radiological attack as described in 13.201(g) (1), except for construction subject to the Davis-Bacon Act (41 U.S.C. 428a)--

(i) $15,000 in the case of any contract to be awarded and performed, or purchase to be made, inside the United States; and

(ii) $25,000 in the case of any contract to be awarded and performed, or purchase to be made outside the United States.

Appendix G
Trade Agreements

Trade Agreements (FAR 52.225-5) (JAN 2005)

(a) Definitions. As used in this clause-

"Caribbean Basin country end product"-

(1) Means an article that-

(i)(A) Is wholly the growth, product, or manufacture of a Caribbean Basin country; or

(B) In the case of an article that consists in whole or in part of materials from another country, has been substantially transformed in a Caribbean Basin country into a new and different article of commerce with a name, character, or use distinct from that of the article or articles from which it was transformed; and

(ii) Is not excluded from duty-free treatment for Caribbean countries under 19 U.S.C. 2703(b).

(A) For this reason, the following articles are not Caribbean Basin country end products:

(1) Tuna, prepared or preserved in any manner in airtight containers;

(2) Petroleum, or any product derived from petroleum;

(3) Watches and watch parts (including cases, bracelets, and straps) of whatever type including, but not limited to, mechanical, quartz digital, or quartz analog, if such watches or watch parts contain any material that is the product of any country to which the Harmonized Tariff Schedule of the United States (HTSUS) column 2 rates of duty apply (i.e., Afghanistan, Cuba, Laos, North Korea, and Vietnam); and

(4) Certain of the following: textiles and apparel articles; footwear, handbags, luggage, flat goods, work gloves, and leather wearing apparel; or handloomed, handmade, and folklore articles;

(B) Access to the HTSUS to determine duty-free status of articles of these types is available at http://www.customs.ustreas.gov/impoexpo/impoexpo.htm. In particular, see the following:

(1) General Note 3(c), Products Eligible for Special Tariff treatment.

(2) General Note 17, Products of Countries Designated as Beneficiary Countries under the United States-Caribbean Basin Trade Partnership Act of 2000.

(3) Section XXII, Chapter 98, Subchapter II, Articles Exported and Returned, Advanced or Improved Abroad, U.S. Note 7(b).

(4) Section XXII, Chapter 98, Subchapter XX, Goods Eligible for Special Tariff Benefits under the United States-Caribbean Basin Trade Partnership Act; and

(2) Refers to a product offered for purchase under a supply contract, but for purposes of calculating the value of the acquisition, includes services (except transportation services) incidental to the article, provided that the value of those incidental services does not exceed that of the article itself.

"Designated country" means any of the following countries:

(1) A World Trade Organization Government Procurement Agreement country (Aruba, Austria, Belgium, Canada, Cyprus, Czech Republic, Denmark, Estonia, Finland, France, Germany, Greece, Hong Kong, Hungary, Iceland, Ireland, Israel, Italy, Japan, Korea (Republic of), Latvia, Liechtenstein, Lithuania, Luxembourg, Malta, Netherlands, Norway, Poland, Portugal, Singapore, Slovak Republic, Slovenia, Spain, Sweden, Switzerland, or United Kingdom);

(2) A Free Trade Agreement country (Australia, Canada, Chile, Mexico, Morocco, or Singapore);

(3) A least developed country (Afghanistan, Angola, Bangladesh, Benin, Bhutan, Burkina Faso, Burundi, Cambodia, Cape Verde, Central African Republic, Chad, Comoros, Democratic Republic of Congo, Djibouti, East Timor, Equatorial Guinea, Eritrea, Ethiopia, Gambia, Guinea, Guinea-Bissau, Haiti, Kiribati, Laos, Lesotho, Madagascar, Malawi, Maldives, Mali, Mauritania, Mozambique,

Nepal, Niger, Rwanda, Samoa, Sao Tome and Principe, Senegal, Sierra Leone, Solomon Islands, Somalia, Tanzania, Togo, Tuvalu, Uganda, Vanuatu, Yemen, or Zambia); or

(4) A Caribbean Basin country (Antigua and Barbuda, Aruba, Bahamas, Barbados, Belize, British Virgin Islands, Costa Rica, Dominica, Dominican Republic, El Salvador, Grenada, Guatemala, Guyana, Haiti, Honduras, Jamaica, Montserrat, Netherlands Antilles, Nicaragua, St. Kitts and Nevis, St. Lucia, St. Vincent and the Grenadines, or Trinidad and Tobago).

"Designated country end product" means a WTO GPA country end product, an FTA country end product, a least developed country end product, or a Caribbean Basin country end product.

"End product" means those articles, materials, and supplies to be acquired under the contract for public use.

"Free Trade Agreement country end product" means an article that-

(1) Is wholly the growth, product, or manufacture of a Free Trade Agreement (FTA) country; or

(2) In the case of an article that consists in whole or in part of materials from another country, has been substantially transformed in an FTA country into a new and different article of commerce with a name, character, or use distinct from that of the article or articles from which it was transformed. The term refers to a product offered for purchase under a supply contract, but for purposes of calculating the value of the end product includes services (except transportation services) incidental to the article, provided that the value of those incidental services does not exceed that of the article itself.

"Least developed country end product" means an article that-

(1) Is wholly the growth, product, or manufacture of a least developed country; or

(2) In the case of an article that consists in whole or in part of materials from another country, has been substantially transformed in a least developed country into a new and different article of commerce with a name, character, or use distinct from that of the article or articles from which it was transformed. The term refers to a product offered

for purchase under a supply contract, but for purposes of calculating the value of the end product, includes services (except transportation services) incidental to the article, provided that the value of those incidental services does not exceed that of the article itself.

"United States" means the 50 States, the District of Columbia, and outlying areas.

"U.S.-made end product" means an article that is mined, produced, or manufactured in the United States or that is substantially transformed in the United States into a new and different article of commerce with a name, character, or use distinct from that of the article or articles from which it was transformed.

"WTO GPA country end product" means an article that-

(1) Is wholly the growth, product, or manufacture of a WTO GPA country; or

(2) In the case of an article that consists in whole or in part of materials from another country, has been substantially transformed in a WTO GPA country into a new and different article of commerce with a name, character, or use distinct from that of the article or articles from which it was transformed. The term refers to a product offered for purchase under a supply contract, but for purposes of calculating the value of the end product includes services, (except transportation services) incidental to the article, provided that the value of those incidental services does not exceed that of the article itself.

(b) Delivery of end products. The Contracting Officer has determined that the WTO GPA and FTAs apply to this acquisition. Unless otherwise specified, these trade agreements apply to all items in the Schedule. The Contractor shall deliver under this contract only U.S.-made or designated country end products except to the extent that, in its offer, it specified delivery of other end products in the provision entitled "Trade Agreements Certificate."

Appendix H – FAR FOB Term Detailed Descriptions

52.247-29 -- F.o.b. – Origin.

As prescribed in 47.303-1(c), insert the following clause:

F.o.b. Origin (Jun 1988)

(a) The term "f.o.b. origin," as used in this clause, means free of expense to the Government delivered --

(1) On board the indicated type of conveyance of the carrier (or of the Government, if specified) at a designated point in the city, county, and State from which the shipment will be made and from which line-haul transportation service (as distinguished from switching, local drayage, or other terminal service) will begin;

(2) To, and placed on, the carrier's wharf (at shipside, within reach of the ship's loading tackle, when the shipping point is within a port area having water transportation service) or the carrier's freight station;

(3) To a U.S. Postal Service facility; or

(4) If stated in the solicitation, to any Government designated point located within the same city or commercial zone as the f.o.b. origin point specified in the contract (commercial zones are prescribed by the Interstate Commerce Commission at 49 CFR 1048).

(b) The Contractor shall --

(1)

(i) Pack and mark the shipment to comply with contract specifications; or

(ii) In the absence of specifications, prepare the shipment in conformance with carrier requirements to protect the goods and to ensure assessment of the lowest applicable transportation charge;

(2)

(i) Order specified carrier equipment when requested by the Government; or

(ii) If not specified, order appropriate carrier equipment not in excess of capacity to accommodate shipment;

(3) Deliver the shipment in good order and condition to the carrier, and load, stow, trim, block, and/or brace carload or truckload shipment (when loaded by the Contractor) on or in the carrier's conveyance as required by carrier rules and regulations;

(4) Be responsible for any loss of and/or damage to the goods --

(i) Occurring before delivery to the carrier;

(ii) Resulting from improper packing and marking; or

(iii) Resulting from improper loading, stowing, trimming, blocking, and/or bracing of the shipment, if loaded by the Contractor on or in the carrier's conveyance;

(5) Complete the Government bill of lading supplied by the ordering agency or, when a Government bill of lading is not supplied, prepare a commercial bill of lading or other transportation receipt. The bill of lading shall show --

(i) A description of the shipment in terms of the governing freight classification or tariff (or Government rate tender) under which lowest freight rates are applicable;

(ii) The seals affixed to the conveyance with their serial numbers or other identification;

(iii) Lengths and capacities of cars or trucks ordered and furnished;

(iv) Other pertinent information required to effect prompt delivery to the consignee, including name, delivery address, postal address and ZIP code of consignee, routing, etc.;

(v) Special instructions or annotations requested by the ordering agency for commercial bills of lading; e.g.,

(A) "To be converted to a Government bill of lading," or

(B) "This shipment is the property of, and the freight charges paid to the carrier(s) will be reimbursed by, the Government"; and

(vi) The signature of the carrier's agent and the date the shipment is received by the carrier; and

(6) Distribute the copies of the bill of lading, or other transportation receipts, as directed by the ordering agency.

(c) These Contractor responsibilities are specified for performance at the plant or plants at which the supplies are to be finally inspected and accepted, unless the facilities for shipment by carrier's equipment are not available at the Contractor's plant, in which case the responsibilities shall be performed f.o.b. the point or points in the same or nearest city where the specified carrier's facilities are available; subject, however, to the following qualifications:

(1) If the Contractor's shipping plant is located in the State of Alaska or Hawaii, the Contractor shall deliver the supplies listed for shipment outside Alaska or Hawaii to the port of loading in Alaska or Hawaii, respectively, as specified in the contract, at Contractor's expense, and to that extent the contract shall be "f.o.b. destination."

(2) Notwithstanding subparagraph (c)(1) of this clause, if the Contractor's shipping plant is located in the State of Hawaii, and the contract requires delivery to be made by container service, the Contractor shall deliver the supplies, at the Contractor's expense, to the container yard in the same or nearest city where seavan container service is available.

(End of Clause)

52.247-30 -- F.o.b. -- Origin, Contractors Facility.

As prescribed in 47.303-2(c), insert the following clause in solicitations and contracts when the delivery term is f.o.b. origin, contractor's facility:

F.o.b. Origin, Contractor's Facility (Apr 1984)

(a) The term "f.o.b. origin, contractor's facility," as used in this clause, means free of expense to the Government delivered on board the indicated type of conveyance of the carrier (or of the Government, if specified) at the designated facility, on the named street or highway, in the city, county, and State from which the shipment will be made.

(b) The Contractor shall --

(1)

(i) Pack and mark the shipment to comply with contract specifications; or

(ii) In the absence of specifications, prepare the shipment in conformance with carrier requirements to protect the goods and to ensure assessment of the lowest applicable transportation charge;

(2)

(i) Order specified carrier equipment when requested by the Government; or

(ii) If not specified, order appropriate carrier equipment not in excess of capacity to accommodate shipment;

(3) Deliver the shipment in good order and condition to the carrier, and load, stow, trim, block, and/or brace carload or truckload shipment (when loaded by the Contractor) on or in the carrier's conveyance as required by carrier rules and regulations;

(4) Be responsible for any loss of and/or damage to the goods --

(i) Occurring before delivery to the carrier;

(ii) Resulting from improper packing and marking; or

(iii) Resulting from improper loading, stowing, trimming, blocking, and/or bracing of the shipment, if loaded by the Contractor on or in the carrier's conveyance;

(5) Complete the Government bill of lading supplied by the ordering agency or, when a Government bill of lading is not supplied, prepare a commercial bill of lading or other transportation receipt. The bill of lading shall show --

(i) A description of the shipment in terms of the governing freight classification or tariff (or Government rate tender) under which lowest freight rates are applicable;

(ii) The seals affixed to the conveyance with their serial numbers or other identification;

(iii) Lengths and capacities of cars or trucks ordered and furnished;

(iv) Other pertinent information required to effect prompt delivery to the consignee, including name, delivery address, postal address and ZIP code of consignee, routing, etc.;

(v) Special instructions or annotations requested by the ordering agency for commercial bills of lading; e.g., --

(A) "To be converted to a Government bill of lading," or

(B) "This shipment is the property of, and the freight charges paid to the carrier(s) will be reimbursed by, the Government"; and

(vi) The signature of the carrier's agent and the date the shipment is received by the carrier; and

(6) Distribute the copies of the bill of lading, or other transportation receipts, as directed by the ordering agency.

(End of Clause)

52.247-31 -- F.o.b. -- Origin, Freight Allowed.

As prescribed in 47.303-3(c), insert the following clause:

F.o.b. Origin, Freight Allowed (Jun 1988)

(a) The term "f.o.b. origin, freight allowed," as used in this clause, means --

(1) Free of expense to the Government delivered --

(i) On board the indicated type of conveyance of the carrier (or of the Government, if specified) at a designated point in the city, county, and State from which the shipments will be made and from which line-haul transportation service (as distinguished from switching, local drayage, or other terminal service) will begin;

(ii) To, and placed on, the carrier's wharf (at shipside within reach of the ship's loading tackle when the shipping point is within a port area having water transportation service) or the carrier's freight station;

(iii) To a U.S. Postal Service facility; or

(iv) If stated in the solicitation, to any Government-designated point located within the same city or commercial zone as the f.o.b. origin point specified in the contract (commercial zones are prescribed by the Interstate Commerce Commission at 49 CFR 1048); and

(2) An allowance for freight, based on applicable published tariff rates (or Government rate tenders) between the points specified in the contract, is deducted from the contract price.

(b) The Contractor shall --

(1)

(i) Pack and mark the shipment to comply with contract specifications; or

(ii) In the absence of specifications, prepare the shipment in conformance with carrier requirements to protect the goods and to ensure assessment of the lowest applicable transportation charge;

(2)

(i) Order specified carrier equipment when requested by the Government; or

(ii) If not specified, order appropriate carrier equipment not in excess of capacity to accommodate shipment;

(3) Deliver the shipment in good order and condition to the carrier, and load, stow, trim, block, and/or brace carload or truckload shipment (when loaded by the Contractor) on or in the carrier's conveyance as required by carrier rules and regulations;

(4) Be responsible for any loss of and/or damage to the goods --

(i) Occurring before delivery to the carrier;

(ii) Resulting from improper packing and marking; or

(iii) Resulting from improper loading, stowing, trimming, blocking, and/or bracing of the shipment, if loaded by the Contractor on or in the carrier's conveyance;

(5) Complete the Government bill of lading supplied by the ordering agency, or when a Government bill of lading is not supplied, prepare a commercial bill of lading or other transportation receipt. The bill of lading shall show --

(i) A description of the shipment in terms of the governing freight classification or tariff (or Government rate tender) under which lowest freight rates are applicable;

(ii) The seals affixed to the conveyance with their serial numbers or other identification;

(iii) Lengths and capacities of cars or trucks ordered and furnished;

(iv) Other pertinent information required to effect prompt delivery to the consignee, including name, delivery address, postal address and ZIP code of consignee, routing, etc.;

(v) Special instructions or annotations requested by the ordering agency for commercial bills of lading; e.g.,

(A) "To be converted to a Government bill of lading," or

(B) "This shipment is the property of, and the freight charges paid to the carrier(s) will be reimbursed by, the Government"; and

(vi) The signature of the carrier's agent and the date the shipment is received by the carrier; and

(6) Distribute the copies of the bill of lading, or other transportation receipts, as directed by the ordering agency.

(c) These Contractor responsibilities are specified for performance at the plant or plants at which the supplies are to be finally inspected and accepted, unless the facilities for shipment by carrier's equipment are not available at the Contractor's plant, in which case the responsibilities shall be performed f.o.b. the point or points in the same or nearest city where the specified carrier's facilities are available; subject, however, to the following qualifications:

(1) If the Contractor's shipping plant is located in the State of Alaska or Hawaii, the Contractor shall deliver the supplies listed for shipment outside Alaska or Hawaii to the port of loading in Alaska or Hawaii, respectively, as specified in the contract, at Contractor's expense, and to that extent the contract shall be "f.o.b. destination."

(2) Notwithstanding subparagraph (c)(1) of this clause, if the Contractor's shipping plant is located in the State of Hawaii, and the contract requires delivery to be made by container service, the Contractor shall deliver the supplies, at the Contractor's expense, to the container yard in the same or nearest city where seavan container service is available.

(End of Clause)

52.247-32 -- F.o.b. -- Origin, Freight Prepaid.

As prescribed in 47.303-4(c), insert the following clause:

F.o.b. Origin, Freight Prepaid (Jun 1988)

(a) The term "f.o.b. origin, freight prepaid," as used in this clause, means --

(1) Free of expense to the Government delivered --

(i) On board the indicated type of conveyance of the carrier (or of the Government, if specified) at a designated point in the city, county, and State from which the shipments will be made and from which line-haul transportation service (as distinguished from switching, local drayage, or other terminal service) will begin;

(ii) To, and placed on, the carrier's wharf (at shipside, within reach of the ship's loading tackle, when the shipping point is within a port area having water transportation service) or the carrier's freight station;

(iii) To a U.S. Postal Service facility; or

(iv) If stated in the solicitation, to any Government-designated point located within the same city or commercial zone as the f.o.b. origin point specified in the contract (commercial zones are prescribed by the Interstate Commerce Commission at 49 CFR 1048); and

(2) The cost of transportation, ultimately the Government's obligation, is prepaid by the contractor to the point specified in the contract.

(b) The Contractor shall --

(1)

(i) Pack and mark the shipment to comply with contract specifications; or

(ii) In the absence of specifications, prepare the shipment in conformance with carrier requirements to protect the goods and to ensure assessment of the lowest applicable transportation charge;

(2)

(i) Order specified carrier equipment when requested by the

Government; or

(ii) If not specified, order appropriate carrier equipment not in excess of capacity to accommodate shipment;

(3) Deliver the shipment in good order and condition to the carrier, and load, stow, trim, block, and/or brace carload or truckload shipment (when loaded by the Contractor) on or in the carrier's conveyance as required by carrier rules and regulations;

(4) Be responsible for any loss of and/or damage to the goods --

(i) Occurring before delivery to the carrier;

(ii) Resulting from improper packing or marking; or

(iii) Resulting from improper loading, stowing, trimming, blocking, and/or bracing of the shipment, if loaded by the Contractor on or in the carrier's conveyance;

(5) Prepare a commercial bill of lading or other transportation receipt. The bill of lading shall show --

(i) A description of the shipment in terms of the governing freight classification or tariff (or Government rate tender) under which lowest freight rates are applicable;

(ii) The seals affixed to the conveyance with their serial numbers or other identification;

(iii) Lengths and capacities of cars or trucks ordered and furnished;

(iv) Other pertinent information required to effect prompt delivery to the consignee, including name, delivery address, postal address and ZIP code of consignee, routing, etc.;

(v) Special instructions or annotations requested by the ordering agency for commercial bills of lading; ***e.g.***, --

(A) "to be converted to a Government bill of lading," or

(B) "this shipment is the property of, and the freight charges paid to the carrier(s) will be reimbursed by, the Government"; and

(vi) The signature of the carrier's agent and the date the shipment is received by the carrier;

(6) Distribute the copies of the bill of lading, or other transportation receipts, as directed by the ordering agency; and

(7) Prepay all freight charges to the extent specified in the contract.

(c) These Contractor responsibilities are specified for performance at the plant or plants at which these supplies are to be finally inspected and accepted, unless the facilities for shipment by carrier's equipment are not available at the Contractor's plant, in which case the responsibilities shall be performed f.o.b. the point or points in the same or nearest city where the specified carrier's facilities are available; subject, however, to the following qualifications:

(1) If the Contractor's shipping plant is located in the State of Alaska or Hawaii, the Contractor shall deliver the supplies listed for shipment outside Alaska or Hawaii to the port of loading in Alaska or Hawaii, respectively, as specified in the contract, at Contractor's expense, and to that extent the contract shall be "f.o.b. destination."

(2) Notwithstanding subparagraph (c)(1) of this clause, if the Contractor's shipping plant is located in the State of Hawaii, and the contract requires delivery to be made by container service, the Contractor shall deliver the supplies, at the Contractor's expense, to the container yard in the same or nearest city where seavan container service is available.

(End of Clause)

52.247-33 -- F.o.b. -- Origin, with Differentials.

As prescribed in 47.303-5(c), insert the following clause:

F.o.b. Origin, with Differentials (Jun 1988)

(a) The term "f.o.b. origin, with differentials," as used in this clause, means --

(1) Free of expense to the Government delivered --

(i) On board the indicated type of conveyance of the carrier (or of the Government, if specified) at a designated point in the city, county, and State from which the shipments will be made and from which line-haul transportation service (as distinguished from switching, local drayage, or other terminal service) will begin;

(ii) To, and placed on, the carrier's wharf (at shipside, within reach of the ship's loading tackle, when the shipping point is within a port area having water transportation service) or the carrier's freight station;

(iii) To a U.S. Postal Service facility; or

(iv) If stated in the solicitation, to any Government-designated point located within the same city or commercial zone as the f.o.b. origin point specified in the contract (commercial zones are prescribed by the Interstate Commerce Commission at 49 CFR 1048); and

(2) Differentials for mode of transportation, type of vehicle, or place of delivery as indicated in Contractor's offer may be added to the contract price.

(b) The Contractor shall --

(1)

(i) Pack and mark the shipment to comply with contract specification; or

(ii) In the absence of specifications, prepare the shipment in conformance with carrier requirements to protect the goods and to ensure assessment of the lowest applicable transportation charge;

(2)

(i) Order specified carrier equipment when requested by the Government; or

(ii) If not specified, order appropriate carrier equipment not in excess of capacity to accommodate shipment;

(3) Deliver the shipment in good order and condition to the carrier, and load, stow, trim, block, and/or brace carload or truckload shipment (when loaded by the Contractor) on or in the carrier's conveyance as required by carrier rules and regulations;

(4) Be responsible for any loss of and/or damage to the goods --

(i) Occurring before delivery to the carrier;

(ii) Resulting from improper packing and marking; or

(iii) Resulting from improper loading, stowing, trimming, blocking, and/or bracing of the shipment, if loaded by the Contractor on or in the carrier's conveyance;

(5) Complete the Government bill of lading supplied by the ordering agency or, when a Government bill of lading is not supplied, prepare a commercial bill of lading or other transportation receipt. The bill of lading shall show --

(i) A description of the shipment in terms of the governing freight classification or tariff (or Government rate tender) under which lowest freight rates are applicable;

(ii) The seals affixed to the conveyance with their serial numbers or other identification;

(iii) Lengths and capacities of cars or trucks ordered and furnished;

(iv) Other pertinent information required to effect prompt delivery to the consignee, including name, delivery address, postal address and ZIP code of consignee, routing, etc.;

(v) Special instructions or annotations requested by the ordering agency for commercial bills of lading; e.g., --

(A) "To be converted to a Government bill of lading," or

(B) "This shipment is the property of, and the freight charges paid to the carrier(s) will be reimbursed by, the Government"; and

(vi) The signature of the carrier's agent and the date the shipment is received by the carrier; and

(6) Distribute the copies of the bill of lading, or other transportation receipts, as directed by the ordering agency.

(c)

(1) It may be advantageous to the offeror to submit f.o.b. origin prices that include only the lowest cost to the Contractor for loading of shipment at the Contractor's plant or most favorable shipping point. The cost beyond that plant or point of bringing the supplies to the place of delivery and the cost of loading, blocking, and bracing on the type vehicle specified by the Government at the time of shipment may exceed the offeror's lowest cost when the offeror ships for the offeror's account. Accordingly, the offeror may indicate differentials that may be added to the offered price. These differentials shall be expressed as a rate in cents for each 100 pounds (CWT) of the supplies

for one or more of the options under this clause that the Government may specify at the time of shipment.

(2) These differential(s) will be considered in the evaluation of offers to determine the lowest overall cost to the Government. If, at the time of shipment, the Government specifies (normally on a Government bill of lading) a mode of transportation, type of vehicle, or place of delivery for which the offeror has set forth a differential, the Contractor shall include the total of such differential costs (the applicable differential multiplied by the actual weight on the Government bill of lading) as a separate reimbursable item on the Contractor's invoice for the supplies.

(3) The Government shall have the option of performing or arranging at its own expense any transportation from Contractor's shipping plant or point to carrier's facility at the time of shipment and, whenever this option is exercised, the Government shall make no reimbursement based on a quoted differential.

(4) Offeror's differentials in cents for each 100 pounds for optional mode of transportation, types of vehicle, transportation within a mode, or place of delivery, specified by the Government at the time of shipment and not included in the f.o.b. origin price indicated in the Schedule by the offeror, are as follows:

_______ (carload, truckload, less-load,
_______ wharf, flatcar, driveaway, etc.)

(End of Clause)

52.247-34 -- F.o.b. – Destination.

As prescribed in 47.303-6(c), insert the following clause:

F.o.b. Destination (Nov 1991)

(a) The term "f.o.b. destination," as used in this clause, means --

(1) Free of expense to the Government, on board the carrier's conveyance, at a specified delivery point where the consignee's facility (plant, warehouse, store, lot, or other location to which shipment can be made) is located; and

(2) Supplies shall be delivered to the destination consignee's wharf (if destination is a port city and supplies are for export), warehouse unloading platform, or receiving dock, at the expense of the Contractor. The Government shall not be liable for any delivery, storage, demurrage, accessorial, or other charges involved before the actual delivery (or "constructive placement" as defined in carrier tariffs) of the supplies to the destination, unless such charges are caused by an act or order of the Government acting in its contractual capacity. If rail carrier is used, supplies shall be delivered to the specified unloading platform of the consignee. If motor carrier (including "piggyback") is used, supplies shall be delivered to truck tailgate at the unloading platform of the consignee, except when the supplies delivered meet the requirements of Item 568 of the National Motor Freight Classification for "heavy or bulky freight." When supplies meeting the requirements of the referenced Item 568 are delivered, unloading (including movement to the tailgate) shall be performed by the consignee, with assistance from the truck driver, if requested. If the contractor uses rail carrier or freight forwarded for less than carload shipments, the contractor shall ensure that the carrier will furnish tailgate delivery, when required, if transfer to truck is required to complete delivery to consignee.

(b) The Contractor shall --

(1)

(i) Pack and mark the shipment to comply with contract specifications; or

(ii) In the absence of specifications, prepare the shipment in conformance with carrier requirements;

(2) Prepare and distribute commercial bills of lading;

(3) Deliver the shipment in good order and condition to the point of delivery specified in the contract;

(4) Be responsible for any loss of and/or damage to the goods occurring before receipt of the shipment by the consignee at the delivery point specified in the contract;

(5) Furnish a delivery schedule and designate the mode of delivering

carrier; and

(6) Pay and bear all charges to the specified point of delivery.

(End of Clause)

52.247-35 -- F.o.b. -- Destination, Within Consignees Premises.

As prescribed in 47.303-7(c), insert the following clause in solicitations and contracts when the delivery term is f.o.b. destination, within consignee's premises:

F.o.b. Destination, Within Consignee's Premises (Apr 1984)

(a) The term "f.o.b. destination, within consignee's premises," as used in this clause, means free of expense to the Government delivered and laid down within the doors of the consignee's premises, including delivery to specific rooms within a building if so specified.

(b) The Contractor shall --

(1)

(i) Pack and mark the shipment to comply with contract specifications; or

(ii) In the absence of specifications, prepare the shipment in conformance with carrier requirements;

(2) Prepare and distribute commercial bills of lading;

(3) Deliver the shipment in good order and condition to the point of delivery specified in the contract;

(4) Be responsible for any loss of and/or damage to the goods occurring before receipt of the shipment by the consignee at the delivery point specified in the contract;

(5) Furnish a delivery schedule and designate the mode of delivering carrier; and

(6) Pay and bear all charges to the specified point of delivery.

(End of Clause)

52.247-36 -- F.a.s. -- Vessel, Port of Shipment.

As prescribed in 47.303-8(c), insert the following clause in solicitations and contracts when the delivery term is f.a.s. vessel, port of shipment:

F.a.s. Vessel, Port of Shipment (Apr 1984)

(a) The term "f.a.s. vessel, port of shipment," as used in this clause, means free of expense to the Government delivered alongside the ocean vessel and within reach of its loading tackle at the specified port of shipment.

(b) The Contractor shall --

(1)

(i) Pack and mark the shipment to comply with contract specifications; or

(ii) In the absence of specifications, prepare the shipment for ocean transportation in conformance with carrier requirements to protect the goods and to ensure assessment of the lowest applicable transportation charge;

(2)

(i) Deliver the shipment in good order and condition alongside the ocean vessel and within reach of its loading tackle, at the point of delivery and on the date or within the period specified in the contract; and

(ii) Pay and bear all applicable charges, including transportation costs, wharfage, handling, and heavy lift charges, if necessary, up to this point;

(3) Provide a clean dock or ship's receipt;

(4) Be responsible for any loss of and/or damage to the goods occurring before delivery of the shipment to the point specified in the contract; and

(5) At the Government's request and expense, assist obtaining the documents required for --

(i) Exportation; or
(ii) Importation at destination.

(End of Clause)

52.247-37 -- F.o.b. -- Vessel, Port of Shipment.

As prescribed in 47.303-9(c), insert the following clause in solicitations and contracts when the delivery term is f.o.b. vessel, port of shipment:

F.o.b. Vessel, Port of Shipment (Apr 1984)

(a) The term "f.o.b. vessel, port of shipment," as used in this clause, means free of expense to the Government loaded, stowed, and trimmed on board the ocean vessel at the specified port of shipment.

(b) The Contractor shall --

(1)

(i) Pack and mark the shipment to comply with contract specifications; or

(ii) In the absence of specifications, prepare the shipment for ocean transportation in conformance with carrier requirements to protect the goods and to ensure assessment of the lowest applicable transportation charge;

(2)

(i) Deliver the shipment on board the ocean vessel in good order and condition on the date or within the period fixed; and

(ii) Pay and bear all charges incurred in placing the shipment actually on board;

(3) Provide a clean ship's receipt or on-board ocean bill of lading;

(4) Be responsible for any loss of and/or damage to the goods occurring before delivery of the shipment on board the ocean vessel; and

(5) At the Government's request and expense, assist in obtaining the documents required for --

(i) Exportation; or
(ii) Importation at destination.

(End of Clause)

52.247-38 -- F.o.b. -- Inland Carrier, Point of Exportation.

As prescribed in 47.303-10(c), insert the following clause in solicitations and contracts when the delivery term is f.o.b. inland carrier, point of exportation:

F.o.b. Inland Carrier, Point of Exportation (Apr 1984)

(a) The term "f.o.b. inland carrier, point of exportation," as used in this clause, means free of expense to the Government, on board the conveyance of the inland carrier, delivered to the specified point of exportation.

(b) The Contractor shall --

(1)

(i) Pack and mark the shipment to comply with contract specifications; or

(ii) In the absence of specifications, prepare the shipment for ocean transportation in conformance with carrier requirements to protect the goods and to ensure assessment of the lowest applicable transportation charge;

(2) Prepare and distribute commercial bills of lading;

(3)

(i) Deliver the shipment in good order and condition in or on the conveyance of the carrier on the date or within the period specified; and

(ii) Pay and bear all applicable charges, including transportation costs, to the point of delivery specified in the contract;

(4) Be responsible for any loss of and/or damage to the goods occurring before delivery of the shipment to the point of delivery in the contract; and

(5) At the Government's request and expense, assist in obtaining the documents required for --

(i) Exportation; or
(ii) Importation at destination.

(End of Clause)

52.247-39 -- F.o.b. -- Inland Point, Country of Importation.

As prescribed in 47.303-11(c), insert the following clause in solicitations and contracts when the delivery term is f.o.b. inland point, country of importation:

F.o.b. Inland Point, Country of Importation (Apr 1984)

(a) The term "f.o.b. inland point, country of importation," as used in this clause, means free of expense to the Government, on board the indicated type of conveyance of the carrier, delivered to the specified inland point where the consignee's facility is located.

(b) The Contractor shall --

(1)

(i) Pack and mark the shipment to comply with contract specifications; or

(ii) In the absence of specifications, prepare the shipment for ocean transportation in conformance with carrier requirements to protect the goods;

(2)

(i) Deliver, in or on the inland carrier's conveyance, the shipment in good order and condition to the specified inland point where the consignee's facility is located; and

(ii) Pay and bear all applicable charges incurred up to the point of delivery, including transportation costs; export, import, or other fees or taxes; costs of landing; wharfage costs; customs duties and costs of certificates of origin; consular invoices; and other documents that may be required for importation; and

(3) Be responsible for any loss of and/or damage to the goods until their arrival on or in the carrier's conveyance at the specified inland point.

(End of Clause)

Appendix I
Example Letter of Supply

OUTLINE FOR COMMITMENT LETTERS

1. Must be on manufacturer's letterhead

2. Must be original letter with original signatures of an officer of the company

3. Must reference the solicitation number

4. Must contain the phrase that the manufacturer is willing to be "a source of supply to the dealer submitting the offer for the term of the contract"

OUTLINE FOR AGENT AUTHORIZATION

In accordance with Federal Acquisition Regulation (FAR) 4.102(e), which states, "when an agent is to sign the contract, other than as stated in paragraphs (a) through (d) of this section, the agent's authorization to bind the principal must be established by evidence satisfactory to the contracting officer."

Please provide the following information on the principal's letterhead:

For Solicitation No. ________________, the undersigned contractor _(principal)_________, hereby authorizes __(agent)___________, to act as agent for the said contractor, with said specific authority delegated from the contractor to the agent. The authority of the agent is limited to exact and specific delegations.

(Check or add desired delegations)

(1) Sign Contracts ____________________________
(2) Negotiate changes ____________________________
(3) Administer orders ____________________________
(4) Receive Payments ____________________________
(5) Other ____________________________

____

Offeror (To be signed only by authorized principal, such as corporate officer of offeror; i.e. may not be signed by sales or purchasing agent, etc)

____________________________ _______________

Title Date

SAMPLE LETTER OF SUPPLY

(This letter may not apply to your particular Schedule. Please check your solicitation to ensure that this sample fits)

(Place on Manufacturer's Letterhead)

RE: **YOUR COMPANY'S NAME**
ADDRESS

Solicitation Number: XXXXXXXXXXXXXX

Letter of Supply

<Manufacturer’s Name> agrees act as a source of supply to the dealer submitting the offer for the term of the contract. **<Manufacturer’s Name>** hereby authorizes **<Company>** to include current and all future products in their GSA Schedule contract.

Commercial Product Certification

<Manufacturer’s Name> certifies that all products proposed for the inclusion on the initial contract or any subsequent contract modifications are newly manufactured products, are regularly used for other Government purposes, and are sold or traded in the course of normal business operations.

Dealer Classification

< Manufacturer’s Name> classifies **<Company>** as a:

[ ] Distributor [ ] Dealer/Reseller [ ] Value Added Reseller

< Manufacturer’s Name> is granting **<Company>** an [ ] exclusive [ ] non exclusive Letter of Supply for this contract.

If issuing a non exclusive, please list who will be receiving or have received Letters of Supply.

Discount to Dealer

The discount being offered the **<Company>** is ______%.

Price Protection

Any products supplied to **<Company>** for the first 12 months of the contract shall be sold to at a cost no higher than the cost at the time the products were included in the initial contract award. The discount ratio from Manufacturer's Suggested Retail Price as specified above will be maintained throughout the Contract period.

Price Reduction Notification

< Manufacturer's Name> agrees to notify **<Company>** no less than 30 days before any of the following:

Reduction of commercial list price of any product listed on a GSA Schedule Contract
Decrease in dealer cost for any product listed on a GSA Schedule Contract
Temporary price reductions, rebates, and/or promotion offered to commercial customers.

Trade Agreements Act Certificate (Deviation) NOT REQUIRED FOR SOME SOLICITATIONS

< Manufacturer's Name> hereby certifies that each end product to be delivered under this contract is a U.S. made end product, a designated country end product, a Caribbean Basin country end product, a Canadian end product, or a Mexican end product as defined in the clause entitled "Trade Agreements Act" at FAR 52.222-9.

Offers will be evaluated in accordance with FAR Subpart 25.4 except that offers of U.S. made end products, designated country end product, a Caribbean Basin country end product, a Canadian end product, or a Mexican end product shall be evaluated without the restrictions of the Buy American Act or the Balance of Payments Program.

Production Point

Contact Name:
Address:
City, State, Zip:
Country:
Phone Number:

Inspection Point

Contact Name:
Address:
City, State, Zip:
Country:
Phone Number:

Sincerely,

<Name of Manufacturer Official> **<Date of Signature>**
<Title of Manufacturer Official>

Appendix J – Sample Subcontracting Plan Format (From the MOBIS Solicitation)

SMALL BUSINESS SUBCONTRACTING PLAN OUTLINE (MODEL)

GSA provides this plan as a tool. It does not establish minimum requirements for an acceptable plan. The model reflects objectives GSA encourages contractors to adopt. GSA expects offerors to thoroughly review the requirements set forth in FAR 19.704, Subcontracting plan requirements, and FAR clause 52.219-9, Small Business Subcontracting Plan, before submitting their contracting plans.

The model is not intended to replace any existing corporate plan which is more extensive. If you need assistance to locate small business sources, contact the Small Business Administration office in your local area or research ProNet on the Internet at http://pro-net.sba.gov. **Please note: Regarding FAR 52.219-9 requirements the following are the targets or goals which offerors should consider and strive to attain when allocating subcontracting effort. It should be noted that these are not mandatory and each offeror's subcontracting goals will vary based upon: (1) his/her approach to satisfying solicitation requirements; and, (2) the available subcontracting opportunities allowed for in the offeror's approach. Goals: 39 % for small business, 3.0% for HUBZone Small Business, 6% for Small Disadvantaged Business (SDB), 5% for Women-Owned Small Business (WOSB), 3% for Service-Disabled Veteran-Owned small businesses for fiscal year 2004-2005.**

Identification Data:
Company Name:______________________________________
Address:____
Date Prepared:_____________Solicitation Number:___________
Item/Service:____

1. TYPE OF PLAN: (Check only one).

____ INDIVIDUAL PLAN: In this type of plan all elements are developed specifically for this contract and apply for the full term of this contract.

____ MASTER PLAN: In this type of plan, goals are separately developed for this contract in an individual plan; all other elements are standard. The master plan must be approved once every three years. Once incorporated into a contract with specific goals, it is valid for the life of the contract.

____ COMMERCIAL PLAN: This type of plan is used when the contractor sells large quantities of off-the-shelf commodities to many Government agencies. Plans and goals are negotiated with the initial agency on a company-wide basis rather than for individual contracts. The plan is effective only during year approved. The contractor must provide a copy of the initial agency approval, and must submit an annual SF 295 to GSA with a breakout of subcontracting prorated for GSA.

2. GOALS:
State separate dollar and percentage goals for small business, HUBZone small, small disadvantaged business, women-owned small business and service- disabled veteran-owned small businesses in the following format. Express all dollar goals as a percentage of total planned subcontracting dollars.

A. Estimated dollar value of all planned subcontracting, i.e., to all types of business concerns under this contract is:

ESTIMATED DOLLAR VALUE OF ALL PLANNED SUBCONTRACTING

BASE	1ST OPTION	2ND OPTION	3RD OPTION
$	$	$	$
100%	100%	100%	100%

B. Estimated dollar value and percentage of total planned subcontracting to large business concerns. (all business concerns classified as other than small)

SUBCONTRACTING TO LARGE BUSINESS CONCERNS

BASE	1ST OPTION	2ND OPTION	3RD OPTION
$	$	$	$
%	%	%	%

C. Estimated dollar value and percentage of total planned subcontracting to small business concerns is: (Include HUBZone Small, Small Disadvantaged, Women-owned Small Business and Service-Disabled Veteran-Owned Small Businesses)

SUBCONTRACTING TO SMALL BUSINESS CONCERNS

BASE	1ST OPTION	2ND OPTION	3RD OPTION
$	$	$	$
%	%	%	%

D. Estimated dollar value and percentage of total planned subcontracting to HUBZone small business concerns is:

SUBCONTRACTING TO HUBZONE SMALL BUSINESS CONCERNS

BASE	1ST OPTION	2ND OPTION	3RD OPTION
$	$	$	$
%	%	%	%

E. Estimated dollar value and percentage of total planned subcontracting to small disadvantaged business concerns is:

SUBCONTRACTING TO SMALL DISADVANTAGED BUSINESS CONCERNS

BASE	1ST OPTION	2ND OPTION	3RD OPTION
$	$	$	$
%	%	%	%

F. Estimated dollar value and percentage of total planned sub-contracting to women-owned small business concerns is:

SUBCONTRACTING TO WOMEN-OWNED SMALL BUSINESS CONCERNS

BASE	1ST OPTION	2ND OPTION	3RD OPTION
$	$	$	$
%	%	%	%

G. Estimated dollar value and percentage of total planned subcontracting to service-disabled veteran-owned small business concerns is:

SUBCONTRACTING TO SERVICE-DISABLED VETERAN OWNED SMALL BUSINESS CONCERN

BASE	1ST OPTION	2ND OPTION	3RD OPTION
$	$	$	$
%	%	%	%

H. Products and/or services to be subcontracted under this contract, and the types of businesses supplying them, are: (Check all that apply).

BUSINESS CATEGORY OR SIZE			
PRODUCT SERVICE	NAICS	LARGE	SMALL BUSINESS

PRODUCT SERVICE	HUB SMALL	SBD	WOSB	SDVO

(Attach additional sheets if necessary.)

H1. Explain the methods used to develop the subcontracting goals for small, HUBZone small, small disadvantaged, women-owned small business concerns and service-disabled veteran-owned small businesses.

H2. Explain how the product and service areas to be subcontracted were established, how the areas to be subcontracted to small, HUBZone small, small disadvantaged, women-owned small business concerns and service-disabled veteran-owned small businesses were determined.

H3. How the capabilities of small, HUBZone small, small disadvantaged, women-owned small business concerns and service-disabled veteran-owned small businesses were determined.

H4. Identify all source lists used in the determination process.

____

____

____

____

____

____

____

I. Indirect and overhead costs __ HAVE BEEN or ___HAVE NOT BEEN included in the dollar and percentage subcontracting goals stated above. (Check one.)

J. If indirect and overhead costs HAVE BEEN included, explain the method used to determine the proportionate share of such costs to be allocated as subcontracts to small, HUBZone small, small disadvantaged, women-owned business concerns and service-disabled veteran-owned small businesses.

____

____

____

____

____

3. PROGRAM ADMINISTRATOR:

FAR 52.219-9(d)(7) requires information about the company employee who will administer the subcontracting program. Please provide the name, title, address, phone number, position within the corporate structure and the duties of that employee.

Name:
Title:
Position:
Address:
Telephone:

Duties: The Program Administrator's general overall responsibility for the Contractor's subcontracting program, i.e., developing, preparing, and executing individual subcontracting plans and monitoring performance relative to this particular plan. These duties may include, but are not limited to the following activities.

A. Developing and promoting company/division policy statements that demonstrate the company's/division's support for awarding contracts and subcontracts to small, HUBZone small, small disadvantaged, women-owned small business concerns and service-disabled veteran-owned small businesses.

B. Developing and maintaining bidders' lists of small, HUBZone small, small disadvantaged, women-owned small business concerns and service-disabled veteran-owned small businesses from all possible sources.

C. Ensuring periodic rotation of potential subcontractors on bidders' lists.

D. Assuring that small, HUBZone small, small disadvantaged, women-owned small business concerns, and service-disabled veteran-owned small businesses are included on the bidders' list for every subcontract solicitation for products and services they are capable of providing.

E. Ensuring that subcontract procurement "packages" are designed to permit the maximum possible participation of small, HUBZone small, small disadvantaged, women-owned small business concerns and service-disabled veteran-owned small businesses.

F. Reviewing subcontract solicitations to remove statements, clauses, etc., which might tend to restrict or prohibit small, HUBZone small, small disadvantaged, women-owned small business and service-disabled veteran-owned small businesses participation.

G. Ensuring that the subcontract bid proposal review board documents its reasons for not selecting any low bids submitted by small, HUBZone small, small disadvantaged, women-owned small business concerns and service-disabled veteran-owned small businesses.

H. Overseeing the establishment and maintenance of contract and subcontract award records.

I. Attending or arranging for the attendance of company counselors at Business Opportunity Workshops, Minority Business Enterprise Seminars, Trade Fairs, etc.

J. Directly or indirectly counseling small, HUBZone small, small disadvantaged women-owned small business concerns and service-disabled veteran-owned small businesses on subcontracting opportunities and how to prepare bids to the company

K. Providing notice to subcontractors concerning penalties for misrepresentations of business status as small, HUBZone small, small disadvantaged, women-owned small business and service-disabled veteran-owned small businesses for the purpose of obtaining a subcontract that is to be included as part or all of a goal contained in the contractor's subcontracting plan.

L. Conducting or arranging training for purchasing personnel regarding the intent and impact of Public Law 95-907 on purchasing procedures.

M. Developing and maintaining an incentive program for buyers which supports the subcontracting program.

N. Monitoring the company's performance and making any adjustments necessary to achieve the subcontract plan goals.

O. Preparing and submitting timely reports.

P. Coordinating the company's activities during compliance reviews by Federal agencies.

4. EQUITABLE OPPORTUNITY

FAR 52.219-9(d)(8) requires a description of the efforts your company will make to ensure that small, HUBZone small, small disadvantaged, women-owned small business concerns and service-disabled veteran-owned small businesses will have an equitable opportunity to compete for subcontracts. These efforts may include, but are not limited to the following activities:

A. Outreach efforts to obtain sources:

____Contacting minority and small business trade associations

____Contacting business development organizations

____Requesting sources from the Small Business Administration's Procurement Marketing and Access Network (PRO-Net).

____Attending small, minority, and women-owned business procurement conferences and trade fairs.

B. Internal efforts to guide and encourage purchasing personnel:

____Presenting workshops, seminars and training programs

____Establishing, maintaining and using small, HUBZone small, small disadvantaged and women-owned business source lists, guides and other data for soliciting subcontracts

____Monitoring activities to evaluate compliance with the subcontracting plan

C. Additional efforts: (Please describe.)

____

____

____

5. CLAUSE INCLUSION AND FLOWDOWN

FAR 52.219-9(d)(9) requires that your company provide assurances that it will include the clause at FAR 52.219-8, "Utilization of Small Business Concerns," in all subcontracts that offer further subcontracting opportunities.

FAR 52.219-9(d)(9) also requires that your company agrees in this plan that it will require all subcontractors, except small business concerns, that receive subcontracts in excess of $500,000 ($1,000,000 for construction) to adopt a plan complies with the requirements of FAR 52.219-9, "Small Business Subcontracting Plan."

(Insert company name) agrees that the clause will be included and that the plans will be reviewed against the minimum requirements for such plans. The acceptability of percentage goals for small, HUBZone small, small disadvantaged, and women-owned small business concerns must be determined on a case-by-case basis depending on the supplies and services involved, the availability of potential small, HUBZone small, small disadvantaged, women-owned small business and service-disabled veteran-owned small businesses subcontractors and prior experience. Once the plans are negotiated, approved, and implemented, the plans must be monitored through the submission of periodic reports, including Standard Form (SF) 294 and SF 295 reports.

In accordance with policy letters published by the Office of Federal Procurement Policy, such assurance must describe the offer's procedures for the review, approval and monitoring for compliance with such subcontracting plans.

6. REPORTING AND COOPERATION

FAR 52.219-9(d)(10) requires that your company (1) cooperate in any studies or surveys as may be required, (2) submit periodic reports which show compliance with the subcontracting plan; (3) submit Standard Form (SF) 294, "Subcontracting Reports for Individual Contracts," and SF 295,

"Summary Subcontract Report," in accordance with the instructions on the forms; and (4) ensure that subcontractors agree to submit SF 294 and SF 295.

Both the Associate Administrator for Enterprise Development and the Small Business Technical Advisor must receive the report(s) within 30 days after the close of each calendar period.

That is:

Calendar Period	Report Due	Date Due	Send Report To
10/01--03/31	SF 294	04/30	Contracting Officer/ Small Business Technical Advisor
04/01--09/30	SF 294	10/30	Contracting Officer/ Small Business Technical Advisor
10/01--09/30	SF 295*	10/30	Contracting Officer/Associate Administrator for Enterprise Development

*SF 295 Must be submitted to SBA's Commercial Market Representative

Small Business Technical Advisor address is: (To Be Completed by Contracting Officer)	Associate Administrator for Enterprise Development address is: (To be completed by Contracting Officer)

<u>7. RECORDKEEPING</u>

FAR 52.219-9(d)(11) requires a list of the types of records your company will maintain to demonstrate the procedures adopted to comply with the requirements and goals in the subcontracting plan.

These records include, but are not limited to, the following:

A. Small, HUBZone small, small disadvantaged, women-owned small business concern and service-disabled veteran-owned small businesses source lists, guides, and other data identifying such vendors.

B. Organizations contacted for small, HUBZone small, small disadvantaged, women-owned small business and service-disabled veteran-owned small businesses sources.

C. On a contract-by-contract basis, records on all subcontract solicitations over $100,000 which indicate for each solicitation:

C1. Whether small business concerns were solicited, and if not, why not.

C2. Whether HUBZone small business concerns were solicited, and if not, why not.

C3. Whether small disadvantaged business concerns were solicited, and if not, why not.

C4. Whether women-owned small business concerns were solicited, and if not, why not.

C5. Whether service-disabled veteran-owned small business concerns were solicited, and if not, why not.

C6. Reasons for the failure of solicited small, small disadvantaged, HUBZone and women-owned small business, service-disabled veteran-owned small business concerns to receive the subcontract award.

D. Records to support other outreach efforts, e.g., contacts with minority and small business trade associations, attendance at small, HUBZone small, minority, women-owned small business and service-disabled veteran-owned small businesses procurement conference and trade fairs.

E. Records to support internal activities to (1) guide and encourage purchasing personnel, e.g., workshops, seminars, training programs, incentive awards; and (2) monitor activities to evaluate compliance.

F. On a contract-by-contract basis, records to support subcontract award data including the name, address and business size of each subcontractor. (This item is not required for company or division-wide commercial plans).

G. Other records to support your compliance with the subcontracting plan: (Please describe)

____

____

____

8. TIMELY PAYMENTS TO SUBCONTRACTORS

FAR 52.219-8(a) requires your company to establish and use procedures to ensure the timely payment of amounts due pursuant to the terms of your subcontracts with small, HUBZone small, small disadvantaged, and women-owned small business concerns.

(Insert company name) has established and uses such procedures:

____

____

____

9. DESCRIPTION OF GOOD FAITH EFFORT

Maximum practicable utilization of small, HUBZone small, small disadvantaged, Women-owned small business and veteran-owned small business concerns as subcontractors in Government contracts is a matter of national interest with both social and economic benefits. When a contractor fails to make a good faith effort to comply with a subcontracting plan, these objectives are not achieved, and 15 U.S.C. 637(d)(4)(F) directs that the contractor must pay liquidated damages. In order to demonstrate your compliance with a good faith effort to achieve the small, HUBZone small, small disadvantaged, women-owned small business and service-disabled veteran-owned small business subcontracting goals, outline the steps your company plans to take. These steps will be negotiated with the contracting officer prior to approval of the plan.

____

____

____

____

The offeror is advised that this subcontracting plan will be made a material part of the contract and that the submission of the SF294 and SF295 will be made a line item deliverable in the contract.

10. SIGNATURES REQUIRED

This subcontracting plan was submitted by:	This subcontracting plan was accepted by:
Signature:	Signature:
Typed Name:	Typed Name:
Title: Date:	Title: Contracting Officer Date:

EZGSA

EZGSA, P.O. Box 30406, Bethesda, Maryland 20824, helps businesses become successful vendors to the federal government by providing consulting services that win Schedules, assure compliance and increase sales; and by presenting jargon-free, industry focused seminars by experts in the field. EZGSA also arranges private seminars fully customized for your company's specific needs and issues, and offers its seminar presentations on CD. For more information, please contact us at handbook@ezgsa.com.

Scott Orbach

Scott Orbach, co-founder and President, EZGSA, has more than 15 years experience in the business consulting and contract management arena. An accomplished speaker, he has developed and conducted a variety of seminars throughout the United States in many areas of government procurement including federal sales, marketing and all aspects of the GSA Schedule process. He is widely sought after as a speaker by embassies, Small Business Associations, Chambers of Commerce, trade associations, trade shows, and other procurement events. Prior to co-founding EZGSA in 1999, Mr. Orbach served as Director of Finance, Controller and Chief Financial Officer at several Washington DC area government contractors, and more recently, as president and co-founder of MidLantic Contract Management, which provides IT, financial, GSA Schedule, Deltek, and DCAA consulting to government contractors. He earned his BA from American University, Kogod College of Business Administration.

Judith Nelson

An accomplished international speaker, most recently invited to speak at a conference in Tel Aviv on management of GSA Schedule contracts, **Judith Nelson** draws from 16 years experience assisting government contractors integrate their commercial business practices and goals with the government's regulations and procurement processes. Ms. Nelson holds a diploma from Georgetown University Institute of Comparative Political and Economic Systems, and was a Harriet S. Truman national finalist for Government Service. She is a member of the GSA IT Industry Government Council (ITIGC) and the National Contract Management Association (NCMA Baltimore-Washington Corridor).

659185

Made in the USA